GEORGE OXFORD MILLER

BACKYARD

SCIENCE &

DISCOVERY

WORKBOOK

CALIFORNIA

ADVENTURE PUBLICATIONS

TABLE OF CONTENTS

ABOUT THIS BOOK

With the highest mountains and the hottest deserts of any state, and 840 miles of Pacific coastline, California contains the greatest number of plant and animal species of any state in the country. The highest point in the Lower 48 states (Mount Whitney, 14,500 feet) and the lowest point in North America (Death Valley, 282 feet below sea level) are only 80 miles apart, so the wonders of nature that you can experience often change rapidly. Every year millions of people travel to California from around the world to see its spectacular mountains, rugged coastline, towering redwood forests, and national parks that rival Disneyland for excitement and adventure. And best of all, the magic and mystery of nature is right here in our home state, and if we look, in our own backyards.

As a nature photographer, environmental journalist, and botanist, I've lived in, written about, and explored California and the Southwest almost all of my life. I spent many memorable summers with my father in Volcano in the Gold Country east of Sacramento. I backpacked magnificent national parks with my children before they could walk, camped with them, and enjoyed their sense of discovery as we hiked through majestic redwoods, panned for gold, and explored rugged coastlines. I believe kids (and adults) need to identify with the outdoors and learn to love the wonders of nature.

This book features **30 hands-on science projects**, such as raising native caterpillars, making mushroom spore prints, attracting moths and other insects with an ultraviolet light; **more than 20 simple, fun introductions** to the region's habitats, birds, seasons, and rocks and minerals; and more than **25 fun activities** to help you make hypotheses, observe nature, and learn about the world around you.

That's really the fun part: you really never know what you're going to find on any given day. It's a little like a treasure hunt, and if you keep good records and share what you find, your observations can even help scientists learn more about the world (or help you start off a career as a scientist).

So get outside, have fun, and share your discoveries!

George Oxford Miller

GEOGRAPHY OF CALIFORNIA

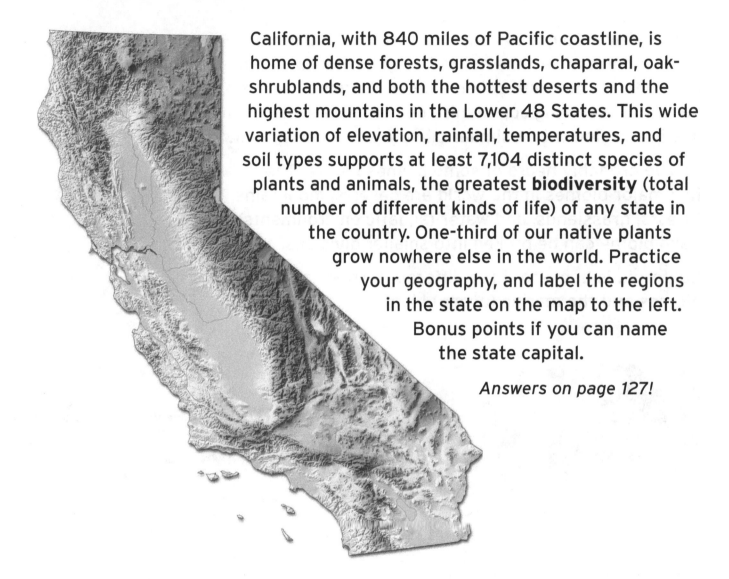

California, with 840 miles of Pacific coastline, is home of dense forests, grasslands, chaparral, oak-shrublands, and both the hottest deserts and the highest mountains in the Lower 48 States. This wide variation of elevation, rainfall, temperatures, and soil types supports at least 7,104 distinct species of plants and animals, the greatest **biodiversity** (total number of different kinds of life) of any state in the country. One-third of our native plants grow nowhere else in the world. Practice your geography, and label the regions in the state on the map to the left. Bonus points if you can name the state capital.

Answers on page 127!

State Capital	Sierra Nevada
Klamath Mountains	Transverse Ranges
Coast Ranges	Peninsula Ranges
Central Valley	Mojave and Sonoran Deserts

GET TO KNOW CALIFORNIA'S BIOMES

The best way to get to know your state—and backyard—is by understanding the natural neighborhoods within its borders: These are called biomes. A **biome** is a large, naturally occurring community of animals and plants that live in a region with a similar climate and environment.

You've probably heard of some biomes before. The five major biomes in the world are deserts, mountains, forests, grasslands, and water (aquatic environments). Each biome can be broken into smaller divisions.

California is home to three different terrestrial (land) biomes and the marine (ocean) biome:

1. Deserts and Dry Shrublands: Cacti, spiny plants, sagebrush (Southern California, Mojave and Colorado Deserts)

2. Temperate Conifer Forests: Pine, redwood, spruce, fir trees (Northern California coast and mountains, Sierra Nevada range)

3. Chaparral Woodlands and Grasslands: Mixture of grasses and shrubs, oaks, pines, and other trees (Coastal southern California, Interior Sierra Nevada foothills; now mostly cities, ranches, and farmland)

4. Marine: Coastal wetlands and Pacific Ocean

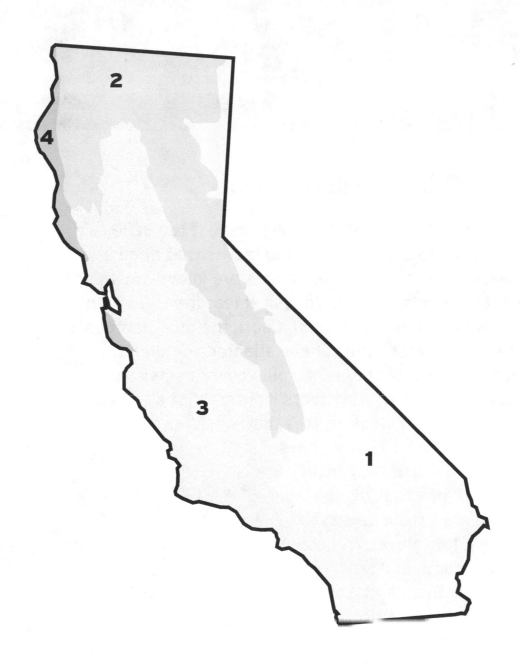

QUICK QUESTION

Which biome do you live in?

_____

_____

_____

DESERTS AND DRY SHRUBLANDS BIOME

Deserts have blazing-hot summers and get too little rain for trees and other plants with big leaves that need a lot of water to survive. Desert plants are known for their many extreme **adaptations** (physical features that help them survive harsh conditions). Cacti, the most famous desert kind of desert plant, have adapted so much that their leaves are now spines. A spiny cover helps shade the juicy stem and also protects it from thirsty animals. Yuccas, like the tall Joshua Tree, have rigid-sword-like leaves. Many desert bushes have tiny leaves that use very little water, and thorny limbs that discourage hungry animals from eating the leaves. Dry, low-elevation deserts have many cacti, and small bushes like Creosote Bush and Catclaw Acacia. Many desert flowers, like the Golden Poppy, don't bloom until it rains, and some seeds can lie **dormant** (like sleeping) in the soil for decades. Then when a good rainy season comes, thousands of seeds **germinate** (begin growing) at the same time and can cover large areas.

Badwater Basin in Death Valley, 282 feet below sea level, is the lowest point in North America.

QUICK QUIZ

Match the plant with its adaptation to survive hot, dry deserts.

A. Flowers wait to bloom until after a big rain

B. Tiny leaves that don't need much water

C. All spines and no leaves

D. Thorny limbs to keep animals from eating leaves

E. Sword-like leaves that animals can't eat

1.

2.

3.

4.

5.

Answers on page 128!

CONIFER FORESTS BIOME

A conifer is a tree that has tiny male cones with pollen instead of showy flowers. Wind blows the pollen to larger female cones, which produce the seeds. Some of the largest conifers, redwoods, have tiny cones. Coniferous forests are common along the northern coast and mountains, and high in the Sierra Nevada range. Among California's conifers are Giant Sequoias, the largest trees in the world, and Coastal Redwoods, which are the tallest. Another is a Bristlecone Pine named Methuselah, which is thought to be the oldest tree in the world at about 5,000 years old.

Conifers like redwoods, pines, firs, yews, and spruce have slender, smooth, needle-like leaves and woody cones. Others, like red-cedars, cypress, and junipers have scale-like leaves in long, braided-like strings. Red-cedars have woody cones while junipers have fleshy, berry-like cones loved by birds. All conifers in California are **evergreen,** which means they don't lose their leaves, or needles, in the winter. Various live oak species and many shrubs are also evergreen. **Deciduous** trees, like cottonwoods, willows, and oaks that grow at lower elevations, lose their leaves in the winter.

FUN FACTS

Tallest tree in the world: "Hyperion," 380 feet—a Coastal Redwood in Redwood National Park

Largest (most massive) tree: "General Sherman," 275 feet tall, 36.5 feet diameter at base, 52,508 cubic feet of wood—a Giant Sequoia in Sequoia National Park.

Oldest tree in the world: "Methuselah," 4,852 years old—a Bristlecone Pine in the White Mountains in Inyo National Forest.

QUICK QUIZ

California is home to 52 species of conifers. Some are ground-hugging and some are over 300 feet tall (that's one football field!).

Can you match these conifer leaves and cones with their trees?

1.

A. Bristlecone Pine

2.

B. Juniper

3.

C. Redwood

4.

D. Spruce

Answers on page 128!

CHAPARRAL WOODLANDS

In California, this bioregion covers much of the coastal woodlands, Central Valley grasslands, and the western slopes of southern mountain ranges. It includes the state's largest cities, from San Francisco south to Los Angeles and San Diego. Shrublands, grasslands, and forests of live oaks and pines grow from the coast into the low coastal mountain ranges.

San Francisco

Most of the region is frost-free all year with occasional inland light freezes. It is considered a **Mediterranean climate**, which occurs in only five areas of the world. It has mild summers and winters, with most of the rain occuring during the winter. The higher elevations have "hard" chaparral with evergreen bushes (they don't lose leaves in winter), while lower elevations have "soft" chaparral with **drought deciduous** plants (they lose their leaves in the dry summers). Chaparral plants are adapted to periodic fires (every 30-100 years), and many need fires to trigger their seeds to germinate (sprout).

As European settlers moved west, they turned the inland valley grasslands into farmland and the coastal chaparral woodlands into large cities. Today, the populations of animals and plants that depended on the chaparral woodlands and grasslands have been greatly reduced. The California Grizzly Bear, which lived in the low mountains and valleys, was hunted to **extinction** in California by 1922. The California Condor, the largest bird in North America, disappeared from the wild in 1987. But after years of captive zoo breeding, a small number have been reintroduced into a few wild locations. Look for them soaring overheard in Big Sur, Bitter Creek National Wildlife Refuge, and Pinnacles National Park.

California Condor

QUICK QUIZ

In the sentence, "The California Grizzly... was hunted to extinction." The word "extinction" means

A. Saved or protected

B. Moved to another area

C. All have been killed or they otherwise no longer exist

D. All have been sent to zoos

Answer on page 128!

MARINE BIOME

Not all forests in California are on land. Giant kelp forests grow just offshore in the marine biome. Oceans cover three-fourths of the world's surface and support an immense number of species of plant and animal life. The **Intertidal Zone**, where the tide washes onto the shore, has a rich and complex web of life. Kelp and other seaweeds, algae, bivalve mollusks (seashells and clams), crabs, sea worms and slugs, and thousands of fishes live in this zone. Gulls patrol the coastline, shorebirds probe the sandy beaches, and the surf washes up seashells along the shoreline.

Estuaries, the wetlands along the coast where freshwater rivers flow into the ocean, are one of the richest zones in the marine biome. The tide brings in nutrients that feed

Seashells wash up on California beaches.

seaweeds and marsh grasses. The small fish, crabs, clams, and other tiny organisms that live here are in turn eaten by larger fishes, gulls, wading birds, otters, seals, and sea lions. In the deeper waters of the bays and open ocean, called the **Pelagic Zone**, whales, dolphins, and large fishes feed on smaller fishes and plankton (tiny shrimp-like creatures). Monterey Bay, San Francisco Bay, and San Diego Bay, and their estuaries, are as rich in sea life as the hills, plains, and mountains are inland life.

Sea lions are common along the California coast.

QUICK QUIZ

In which zone in the marine biome would you most likely see each of these animals?

A. Whales _____

B. Seals and sea lions_____

C. Animals that live in seashells _____

Answers on page 128!

THEN VS. NOW

Before settlers arrived in California and began mining gold, grazing cattle, and cutting timber, numerous groups of Native Americans lived on the bounties of nature: fish from the bays and rivers, fruit and acorns from the foothill woodlands, and wild game. Eventually, the small towns settled by the newcomers grew into cities and then into huge metropolises with millions of people. Naturally, most people wanted to live along the coast where the winters were mild, bays provided safe harbors for ships, and valleys could be farmed all year.

San Diego

Today, most of the coastal chaparral woodlands in the southern half the state, and the plants and animals that

Coastal Redwood trunk

lived there, have been replaced by cities. Farmers harvest crops year-round in the grasslands and valleys, and sawmills have cut 96 percent of the redwood forests. Over thousands of years, the grasses and shrubby plants of the chaparral adapted to survive long droughts and frequent wildfires that periodically sweep across the hills and valleys. Today, wildfire is an ever-present danger to the people and towns in areas where wildfires naturally occur. Due to population growth and loss of habitat, about 250 species of plants and animals in California are threatened with extinction.

QUICK QUIZ

Which animals used to be common in large parts of California but are now rare or absent altogether?

A. California Condor

B. Bighorn Sheep

C. Desert Tortoise

D. Gray Wolf

E. California Grizzly Bear

F. All of them

Answer on page 128!

Grizzly Bear

CALIFORNIA STATE SYMBOLS

Another good way to get to know the region is by learning which plants, animals, and natural materials are California's state symbols. From the state bird and flower, which you might know already, to lesser-known categories, such as state amphibian, gemstone, or fossil, these symbols are usually selected because they have a long history with the state.

QUICK QUIZ

California, called "The Golden State," is rich in mineral resources. Which of the state symbols could you use to make fine jewelry?

A. Gold

B. Benitoite

C. Serpentine

D. All of them

Answer on page 128!

Dome of California's State Capitol building in Sacramento

California Valley Quail

Bird

Golden Poppy

Flower

California Grizzly Bear

Animal

Augustynolophus morrisi

Dinosaur

Saber-toothed Cat

Fossil

Desert Tortoise

Reptile

California Dog-face Butterfly

Insect

California Redwood

Tree

Benitoite

Gemstone

Native Gold

Mineral

Serpentine

Rock

INTRODUCED VS. INVASIVE

Over the course of the settlement of California, many plants and animals were **introduced** to the region. Some of these, such as apples, peaches, tomatoes, and cows, were introduced on purpose; they are **nonnative**, but haven't been a problem. Others that were introduced on purpose or accidentally spread quickly, often finding an environment with few **predators** or natural checks on their population.These species then became **invasive**, spreading uncontrollably and hurting native animals and plants.

A few familiar, but invasive, species:

American Bullfrog

Domestic Honeybee

Yellow Starthistle

Bull Thistle

Starling

House Sparrow

Pigeon

QUICK QUIZ

Which of the following animals is an introduced species in California?

A. Mountain Lion   B. Jackrabbit   C. Coyote   D. Cow

Answer on page 128!

Can you think of other introduced species in your area?
Hint: Most farm animals aren't from here! The same is
true for many weeds.

_____

_____

_____

_____

_____

_____

_____

_____

GETTING TO KNOW YOUR WEATHER

You know it gets really hot in the summer, but what's the hottest temperature you can remember? One hundred degrees, maybe 110? What do you think is the highest temperature recorded anywhere in the state? **Note:** It may not have reached this temperature where you live, but it did happen somewhere in the state.

MAKE A HYPOTHESIS

1. Highest maximum temperature in my state?

_____

_____

2. OK, and you've felt cold, too, maybe shivering at the bus stop or walking to school. So what do you think the coldest temperature recorded anywhere in your state is?

_____

_____

3. And do you like making a snowman or having snowball fights? Or how about sledding down slopes or snowshoeing. Me too. Coastal California has warm winters and no snow, but the forests and mountains get lots of snow. What do you think the record is for the deepest snow on the ground anywhere in your state? A foot? Ten feet? More?

_____

_____

A FEW CALIFORNIA WEATHER RECORDS

HIGHEST TEMPERATURE RECORD

Location	Temp (°F)	Date
Death Valley National Park	130°	August 2020
Eureka	87°	September 2020
San Francisco	106°	September 2017
Los Angeles	113°	September 2010
San Diego	111°	September 1963

COLDEST TEMPERATURE RECORD

Location	Temp (°F)	Date
Boca	-45°	January 1937
Eureka	21°	December 1972
San Francisco	27°	December 1932
Los Angeles	28°	January 1949
San Diego	25°	January 1913

IS THE SUN SETTING EARLIER?!

In winter, you've probably noticed how it gets darker earlier. That happens because Earth is tilted on its axis, so certain parts of the planet get more daylight in some seasons than in others. If you've traveled very far north from where you live, you've probably noticed that the amount of daylight varies with **latitude** (how far north or south you are from the equator).

MAKE A HYPOTHESIS

1. What month do you think has the shortest day of the year in California?

_____

2. Which month has the longest day of the year in California?

_____

3. On the shortest day of the year where you live, what time is sunset?

_____

4. On the longest day of the year where you live, what time is sunset?

_____

LONGEST & SHORTEST DAYS ACROSS CALIFORNIA

The longest day of the year is known as the **summer solstice**; in the Northern Hemisphere that's when the North Pole is tilted the most toward the sun. The shortest day is known as the **winter solstice**; in the Northern Hemisphere that's when the North Pole is tilted the most away from the sun. At the summer solstice, the sun never goes below the horizon at the North Pole (24 hours of daylight), and at the winter solstice, the sun never rises (24 hours of night). At the **equator,** (the line around the Earth halfway between the North and South Poles) the days and nights are equal all year, at 12 hours each.

The date of each solstice varies a little each year. In the Northern Hemisphere, the half of the Earth north of the equator, the summer solstice always occurs between June 20 and June 22, and the winter solstice between December 20 and December 23.

In an upcoming solstice, the times to the right are when the sun will rise and set at the winter and summer solstice in several cities across California. The first is in the far north of the state, the middle two are in the middle, and the fourth city is in the far southern portion of the state. Notice how much longer the days are in the summer than in the winter. Hooray for long summer days!

Source: esrl.noaa.gov/gmd/grad/solcalc

WINTER SOLSTICE

Eureka
December 21
Sunrise: 7:37 am
Sunset: 4:52 pm

San Francisco
December 21
Sunrise: 7:21 am
Sunset: 4:54 pm

Los Angeles
December 21
Sunrise: 6:54 am
Sunset: 4:47 pm

San Diego
December 21
Sunrise: 6:47 am
Sunset: 4:46 pm

SUMMER SOLSTICE

Eureka
June 20
Sunrise: 5:45 am
Sunset: 8:51 pm

San Francisco
June 20
Sunrise: 5:47 am
Sunset: 8:34 pm

Los Angeles
June 20
Sunrise: 5:41 am
Sunset: 8:07 pm

San Diego
June 20
Sunrise: 5:41 am
Sunset: 7:59 pm

AVERAGE FIRST & LAST FROST DATES

Anxious to plant your garden? Well, before you get out and start planting, you have to keep the temperature in mind. If it drops below freezing (especially overnight), the water within the plants will freeze, and cold-sensitive plants can be damaged, or even killed. (This is called a **killing frost.**) This is why gardeners don't plant anything until the danger of a frost has passed.

California farms grow most of the lettuce that feeds the nation.

Here are the approximate dates of the last and first frosts across California. Along the coast and central valleys, the temperature rarely or never drops below freezing. If you live in these regions, you can grow gardens and crops almost year-round.

- **Eureka:**
  Last frost: February 13
  First frost: December 7
  Growing season: 302 days

- **San Francisco:**
  Last frost: January 24
  First frost: December 14
  Growing season: 325 days

- **Los Angeles:**
  Frost free all year
  Growing season: 365 days

- **San Diego:**
  Frost free all year
  Growing season: 365 days

Farmers markets sell fresh produce straight from the farmer to you.

GET TO KNOW THE SEASONS & THE WEATHER

In California, the Pacific coastline and the rapid change in elevation going up the slopes of the Coast Ranges are major factors that determine the climate and seasons. Moisture pouring in from the Pacific creates a Mediterranean climate with mild, dry summers and cool, wet winters. The towering Sierra Nevada Mountains create a **rain shadow**, a wall that blocks the Pacific moisture from flowing over the high peaks. The lack of moisture on the east sides of the ridges creates the Mojave Desert. Death Valley in the Mojave Desert is one of the hottest and driest places on the planet.

Like the daily clock tells us when to get up and go to school, the changes in the seasons during the year tell animals and plants what to do. Day length, temperature, rain and snow, and other weather conditions tell plants

Rain and fog from the Pacific Ocean nourish the plants along the coast of California.

when to start growing leaves and flowers and set seeds. That's how animals know when to breed, migrate, or hibernate. The timing of many of these conditions varies slightly from year to year and decade to decade.

The study of the seasonal cycles of plants and animals is called **phenology.** By observing the phenology of your area—when migrating birds arrive in spring or flowers start to bloom, or when trees drop their leaves in the fall—you'll learn a lot about the natural world around you and what to expect next.

Melting snow in the spring triggers many flowers to sprout and bloom.

YOUR PERSONAL PHENOLOGY

What time do you go to school in the morning? _____

What time do you eat lunch? _____

What month is school out for summer vacation? _____

What month do you open birthday presents?_____

START OUT BY MAKING SOME PREDICTIONS

Before you start observing, see what you already know. Make some predictions about when you expect to see the birds, wildlife, and flowers around you. You might not have seen all of these animals or plants before. If not, that's OK, but make predictions about those you recognize.

Many birds breed in the Canadian forests and Arctic regions. The huge hatch of insects in the summer give the birds lots of food for their babies. But in the frigid winter they have to leave and fly south to warmer areas where they can find food. Many water birds spend their

GET TO KNOW THE SEASONS & THE WEATHER

Every spring and fall, Gray Whales migrate between Alaska and Mexico along the coast of California.

winter, in marshlands along the warm California coast. Most songbirds continue flying south along the coast into Mexico and beyond. The California coastline between the ocean and inner mountains is part of the **Pacific Flyway**. Each year, millions of birds follow the flyway north in the spring and south in the fall. Gray Whales and Humpback Whales also leave the Arctic waters in the winter and swim thousands of miles to the warmer waters along the California and Mexico coast.

Most hummingbirds in the West migrate to Mexico and farther south for the winter. They return to their breeding grounds in the United States and Canada in the spring when flowers, their primary food source, begin to bloom. If you hang up a sugar-water feeder in your yard, hummingbirds will probably come to feed.

QUICK QUIZ

1. What month do you first see hummingbirds in your yard or in nature?

_____

2. What two seasons do gray whales migrate along the coast?

_____

3. Which month do Golden Poppies start blooming where you live?

_____

4. Wildflowers grow in natural areas, like hillsides, and disturbed areas, like roadsides. What month do you see the first wildflowers?

_____

5. Do you have a tree (or a bush) in your yard or nearby that has showy flowers? What month do the flowers begin to bloom?

_____

6. Do you have cacti where you live? If so, what month do they start to bloom?

_____

7. In the winter, the western population of Monarch butterflies migrates to the California coast between Mendocino and San Diego. What month do you see the first Monarch?

_____

Broad-Tailed Hummingbird

Gray Whale

Purple Pricklypear

Monarch Butterfly

BACKYARD PHENOLOGY

The easiest way to start out with phenology is by observing one type of plant or animal throughout the year. It's easiest to start in your yard. Some trees and shrubs are deciduous, meaning they lose their leaves in the winter (or some during summer droughts). Others are evergreen, meaning they always have green leaves. If you have a flowering or fruiting tree or shrub in your yard or nearby, keep track of the seasonal cycle: when the buds emerge in the spring, flowers form, fruit (seeds) develops, and when the seeds or fruit get ripe. Jot down a few notes about the weather, too, since rain and temperature are some of the main triggers for what happens in nature. When you start observing the cycle of plants and animals, keep track of things on a form like this:

Date:_____

Plant: _____

Buds form: _____

Flowers form: _____

Leaves on deciduous tree or shrub emerge:_____

Deciduous tree or shrub is fully "leafed out": _____

Seeds or fruit get ripe:_____

All deciduous leaves have fallen from tree: _____

Try to make a habit of making regular observations and keeping them in a notebook, so you can compare what you see year after year. Does the tree have buds the same day of each year? How about seeds? What was the weather like?

Date:_____

Plant: _____

Buds form: _____

Flowers form: _____

Leaves on deciduous tree or shrub emerge:_____

Deciduous tree or shrub is fully "leafed out": _____

Seeds or fruit get ripe:_____

All deciduous leaves have fallen from tree: _____

California Buckeye: Some deciduous trees like the California Buckeye lose their leaves during the dry summer.

PHENOLOGY CALENDAR: SPRING

Certain natural events tend to happen around the same time each year. Such events can vary each year, especially by location, so keeping track of when you spot plants, animals, and natural events is a great way to really get to know nature in your area.

MARCH

- Wildflowers are blooming in northern California
- Butterflies are active
- Bumblebees start visiting flowers
- Many cacti start blooming
- Dragonflies start flying around water
- Mice and other small mammals have first litter of babies
- Great Horned Owls eggs hatch
- Black bears emerge from winter dens
- Songbirds are active
- Strong hot, dry Santa Ana winds stop blowing across southern California

What I spotted in March:

_____

_____

_____

_____

_____

_____

Acmon Blue Butterfly

Great Horned Owl

Black bear

APRIL

- Joshua Tree and other yuccas are blooming
- Cholla cacti are blooming
- Lesser Goldfinches build nests
- Snakes and lizards become active on hot days
- Hummingbirds are active at backyard feeders
- Migrant songbirds pass through, heading north
- Peak strawberry season (through August)

What I spotted in April:

_____

_____

_____

_____

_____

_____

_____

_____

_____

Yucca

Lesser Goldfinch

Rattlesnake

Strawberries

Source for all phenology data: www.usanpn.org/data

MAY

- Sunflowers are blooming
- Deer give birth to 1-2 fawns
- Mountain and Western Bluebirds start building nests in tree cavities or nest boxes
- Rivers reach peak flow from snowmelt runoff
- Peaches ready to harvest (through September)
- Cherries ready to pick

What I spotted in May:

_____

_____

_____

_____

_____

_____

_____

_____

_____

_____

Deer

Mountain Bluebird

Sunflower

Peaches

Cherries

PHENOLOGY CALENDAR: SUMMER

JUNE

- Temperatures reach 100° F. in deserts
- Sweet corn ready to harvest
- Tomatoes ready to pick
- Milkweeds have flowers

What I spotted in June:

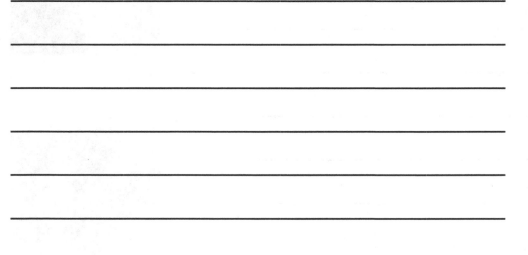

_____

_____

_____

_____

_____

_____

_____

_____

_____

Tomatoes

Milkweed

Desert sand dunes

JULY

- Alpine flowers begin to bloom
- Apples ready to pick
- Grapes ready to harvest
  (through December)

AUGUST

- Goldenrod flowers peak blooming
- Apples ready to pick
- Almonds and other nuts ready
  to harvest

What I spotted in July and August:

_____

_____

_____

_____

_____

_____

_____

_____

_____

Alpine wildflowers

Apples

Grapes

Goldenrod

Almonds

PHENOLOGY CALENDAR: FALL

SEPTEMBER

- Bees busy filling nest burrows with pollen before winter
- Flowers and grass have lots of seeds
- Birds that migrate eat a lot to build up fat reserves for long flight
- Songbirds and hawks migrating to Mexico fly south along the coast
- Corn mazes and u-pick-'em pumpkin patches open for business
- Male deer (bucks) grow their antlers

Bumblebee

Grass seeds

What I spotted in September:

_____

_____

_____

Pumpkins

_____

_____

_____

Deer

_____

_____

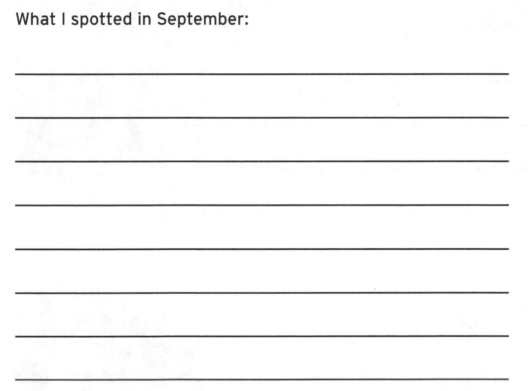

OCTOBER

- Monarch butterflies begin massing along the coast for winter
- Many hummingbirds begin migrating south
- Strong hot, dry Santa Ana winds start blowing across southern California
- Cottonwood, maple, and aspen tree leaves turn colors
- Average first snowfall on high mountain peaks

NOVEMBER

- Small mammals like chipmunks and ground squirrels begin hibernation
- Insects like bees and some butterflies begin hibernation
- Black bears enter dens for winter dormancy
- Snakes and lizards begin hibernation in rocky places and old burrows

What I spotted in October and November:

_____

_____

_____

_____

_____

_____

_____

_____

Monarch Butterflies

A rattlesnake and its burrow

Chipmunk

Aspens

PHENOLOGY CALENDAR: WINTER

DECEMBER

- First month of winter
- Heavy snow in high mountains
- Animal tracks easy to see in snow

Snow in mountains

Leafless Aspens

JANUARY

- Coldest month in Sierra Nevada, with average low temperatures of 3-15° F.
- Rainiest month for entire state
- Black bear cubs born in winter dens
- Oranges and other citrus fruits ready to pick in the south

Oranges

FEBRUARY

- Last month of winter
- Dandelions start flowering in lawns
- Golden Poppies start blooming in deserts
- Great Horned Owls begin nesting
- Monarch butterflies begin migrating north from their coastal refuges
- Deciduous trees begin to bud

What I spotted in the winter:

Golden Poppies

_____

_____

_____

_____

YOUR STATE'S MAJOR FARM CROPS & FARM PRODUCTS

After settlement by Spanish and American colonists, much of California became farms and rangeland for cattle. With a year-round growing season for many vegetables, and the ideal climate for nut trees like almonds and walnuts and fruit trees like oranges and lemons, California farmers literally feed much of the entire nation. The long growing season for grasses provides rich pastureland, making cattle and dairy the number one commodity (agricultural product) in the state.

These are the top ten crops or **commodities** for the year 2019 in California.

Flowers
$1.22 billion

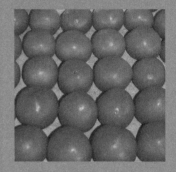
Tomatoes
$1.17 billion

Dairy Products, Milk
$7.34 billion

Almonds
$6.09 billion

Grapes
$5.41 billion

Cattle and calves
$3.06 billion

Strawberries
$2.22 billion

Pistachios
$1.94 billion

Lettuce
$1.82 billion

Walnuts
$1.29 billion

QUICK QUIZ

California grows 99 percent of the table grapes and pistachio nuts in the US, as well as 90 percent of the lettuce and tomatoes, and 80 percent of the citrus fruits. List how many of the top ten commodities you eat in a typical day.

1. _____

2. _____

3. _____

4. _____

5. _____

Farmers Market

GETTING TO KNOW THE FOOD SUPPLY CHAIN

Farmers not only have to grow the crops, they have to get them from the fields to the grocery stores. If you live in an area with lots of farmland, probably most of the fresh fruit and veggies you eat are grown nearby. But many food items must travel a long way, and be peeled, cooked, canned, or frozen. They're stored in warehouses and delivered to stores before they finally reach your table.

Got milk? Got a burger? Did you ever wonder where all the ingredients in a hamburger come from? How did the restaurant get the buns, lettuce, tomatoes, mayonnaise and beef patty? And where did the milk and ice cream for your milkshake come from? Sure, they bought them from a store, just like your parents buy the groceries you eat, but where did the store get them? You can trace each step all the way back to a farmer or rancher who starts

Tractor at work

the whole process. Each step is like a link in a chain. If one "link" breaks, the whole supply line fails, and we can't order your burger.

Many things can break the food supply chain and threaten the delivery of the food we eat. Pandemics like COVID, drought, wildfires, floods and not enough farm workers can make getting food difficult. The next time you go to a grocery store, farmers market, or restaurant, think about the long journey that each item must take from the farm to the table.

Pumpkins ripen in late summer.

QUICK QUIZ

Which of the following are necessary to get food from the farm to your table?

A. Truck drivers

B. Tractors

C. Grocery stores

D. Farm workers

E. All of the above

Answer on page 128!

WHAT'S THE HIGHEST & LOWEST POINT IN THE STATE?

California has the tallest, snow-capped mountain peaks in the Lower 48, as well as one of the lowest spots in the world. Broad valleys bordered by towering mountain ranges run through the central part of the state. Death Valley, in the scorching Mojave Desert, is below sea level. When measuring a location's elevation, like a city or mountaintop, geographers compare it to sea level. For example, the coast of California is at zero feet at the Pacific Ocean.

What do you think the highest point is in your state? What about the lowest?

Highest: _____ feet above sea level

Lowest: _____ feet below sea level

FAST FACT

Visiting the highest point in a state or area is a growing hobby. Known as "high-pointing," it's a fun way to get to explore your state and discover its quirks. Though in some places, such as mountain peaks surrounded by wilderness, or here in California where the highest point is more than 14,000 feet high, you'll definitely need a lot of experience, gear, and training before you ever make an attempt.

Source: www.usgs.gov/science-support/osqi/yes/resources-teachers/highest-and-lowest-elevations

Highest Point in California: **14,500 feet above sea level**

Mount Whitney

Lowest Point in California: **282 feet below sea level**

Death Valley

SPOT YOUR STATE BIRD

CALIFORNIA VALLEY QUAIL

WHEN WILL I SEE THEM?

The California Valley Quail is a chunky bird with a black throat, scale-like feathers on its belly, and a showy topknot (feathers on top of head). They live in low, scrubby vegetation from the coast into the foothills and valleys. Large flocks, called coveys, scratch around on the ground feeding on seeds, tender leaves, acorns, berries, and insects. They lay 10–15 eggs in a rough nest on the ground under a bush or brush pile. Unlike songbird chicks that take weeks to grow feathers and learn to feed themselves, quail chicks leave the nest the day they hatch and follow their parents around searching for food. Listen for their cackling three-note call, with the second note the highest.

WILL THEY COME TO MY YARD?

Maybe, if you live where they naturally are nearby. Scatter grain or birdseed on the ground, and always keep pet cats inside. Quail need low, dense shrubs for protection and nesting sites.

MAKE YOUR YARD BIRD-FRIENDLY

Lawns are pretty and gravel landscapes easy to maintain, but they don't do a lot to help birds, butterflies, bees, and most other kinds of wildlife. To really attract birds (and the insects they eat!), you need to start from the ground up to make your yard a bit wilder. It's pretty easy to start doing this. Here are a few tips to get going:

PLANT NATIVE PLANTS

When you're planting native trees and shrubs to provide cover, nesting sites, and fruit, or wildflowers for pollen, nectar, and seeds, remember that native plants are beacons to birds. Choose a plant that starts blooming in the early spring and produces nectar and seeds throughout the summer and fall. For a list of what to plant, see helpful books on native plant gardening, like *Native Plant Gardening for Birds, Bees & Butterflies: Southern California*, and websites like Calscape. org and allaboutbrds.org/. To make sure you're finding the best native plants, look for a native plant nursery near you. You can see examples of different plants at one of the many public gardens in California.

PUT OUT A WATER SOURCE

Birds don't just need food. They need water too! A bird bath is an easy option, or you can get a small solar-powered fountain with water pouring through several bowls. The sound of the moving water draws in birds from all over.

Bird bath with robins

MAKE YOUR YARD BIRD-FRIENDLY

PROTECTION

Birds are easily scared and have learned to fly away if they feel threatened. A bird-friendly yard has plenty of places where a bird can feel safe, like a thick bush or tree where they can hide or sit in the shade when they're not feeding.

DON'T SPRAY YOUR YARD WITH BUG OR WEED KILLERS

Sometimes caterpillars, beetles, or aphids (tiny, juice-sucking bugs) may attack your plants, but resist spraying poisons. Birds love to eat caterpillars, which turn into beautiful butterflies and neat moths. Small birds and lady bug beetles eat aphids. And those weeds—many are host plants for caterpillars. In a yard, you can often pull the weeds and pick harmful insects off the plants, or use soapy water in a spray bottle. Broad-spectrum insecticides and herbicides can kill any bugs or plants they touch, including the ones you want in your yard.

QUICK QUIZ

What do you need in your yard to make it bird-friendly?

A. Water

B. Food

C. Thick bushes for shelter and protection

D. All of the above

Answer on page 128!

Ladder-backed Woodpecker

Milkweed

White-winged Dove

Dark-eyed Junco

LEAVE OUT NEST-MAKING MATERIALS IN SPRING

Bird nests are pretty incredible, and it's even more impressive that birds make them using only their feet and their beaks!

WHAT TO DO

You can help them out by leaving natural, pesticide-free nesting materials in handy locations around your yard. Examples include soft, fluffy plant parts, such as the down from cattails or milkweeds, small twigs, clumps of grass blades, moss, or feathers you find on the ground (but make sure to wear gloves when picking those up). Remember, birds want their nests to blend in with the surrounding leaves so predators can't find their eggs. You can put these in easy-to-access places around your yard, on the ground, wedged into tree bark, or even hanging in an empty suet feeder.

Important Note: There are some things you don't want to give birds, especially synthetic (man-made) materials such as plastic, metal, or lint. These can be **toxic** (poisonous) to birds, either if they eat some of these things or if they absorb some of the chemicals in them.

Cattail fluff is often used in bird nests.

MAKE A RECIPE TO FEED TO BIRDS

Often birdseed mixes in stores contain a lot of filler seeds that most backyard birds won't eat. Avoid mixes loaded with red or golden millet, cracked corn, wheat, and flaxseed—most songbirds will pitch those out onto the ground. Look for premium mixes where the first ingredients include black oil sunflower seeds (best), striped sunflower seeds, white proso millet, safflower, and milo seeds. If seed-shell litter is a problem, a more expensive solution is to buy mixes with shelled sunflower seeds, or mix your own.

Beside a feeder with a seed mixture, add a thistle or nyjer seed feeder and the Lesser Goldfinches and House Finches will mob the scene, and native sparrows, doves, juncos, and towhees clean up the spillage on the ground. The small openings in a thistle feeder or sock discourages House Sparrows.

Every yard needs a hummingbird feeder, or several. Mixing sugar water is easy: Fill a measuring cup with one cup hot water and add ¼ cup white sugar; stir until dissolved. Be sure to change sugar water and clean the feeder weekly, or more often in hot weather, to prevent fermented water and fungus.

If you get creative, you can feed birds a lot more than birdseed! Making your own bird food is a fun way to attract the birds you want to see. Here are two options for homemade mixes, though there are lots of others.

DO-IT-YOURSELF-BIRD-MIX

Base mix

- 4 cups black oil sunflower seed
- 1 cup white proso millet
- 1 cup safflower seed
- 1 cup milo

Optional

- substitute hulled sunflower seeds to reduce hull litter below feeder
- add 1 cup chipped peanuts

SUET WINTERTIME TREAT

Winter birds thrive on high-calorie suet, but offer it only when it's cold enough (daytime below 60° F.) to keep the mix from melting or becoming rancid. Have an adult heat the lard in a pot until melted, and slowly stir in other ingredients. Pour into shallow pie dishes, tuna cans, or ice cube trays and cool. Place a suet dish on a tray feeder or cubes in a suet feeder, or pack suet into feeder logs with holes, or in pine cones to hang from limbs.

• 1 pound lard

• 1 pound crunchy peanut butter

• 1½ cup cornmeal

• 1½ cup quick oats

• ⅓ cup sugar

Optional

• 1½ cups raisins

• 1½ cups seeds (sunflower or seed mix)

Make both kinds of feeders, then keep track of the birds that come to each one! Did different birds come to the different feeders?

_____

_____

_____

_____

DO A BACKYARD BIRD COUNT

If you're new to birding, chances are you probably haven't conducted a backyard bird count before. It's a simple activity, but it can teach you quite a bit about birds, including how to recognize their calls and when and where to look. It's also a lot of fun, and you might be surprised at what you find. Best of all, you don't need any gear at all, though a field guide, binoculars, and a smartphone camera are handy.

WHAT YOU WILL NEED

• A notepad and a pen, to record your finds

• A field guide, binoculrs, and a smartphone camera (optional)

WHAT TO DO

To conduct your count, get your notebook and pick a 15-minute time slot to look for birds. Go to your backyard, balcony, or a nearby park and quietly look and listen for birds. Look near feeders and birdbaths, if you have them; see if you can spy birds flitting about in cover or perched in trees, and especially near garden areas (even potted plants or container gardens).

Wherever you are, but especially in the city or the suburbs, look for birds soaring overhead. The cities might not seem like birding hotspots, but major cities usually have rivers and parks and shady neighborhoods. Places with gatherings of pigeons and other birds are often home to Cooper's Hawks and kestrels.

When someone spots a bird, point it out—again, quietly—and try to snag a zoomed-in shot. (It doesn't have to be perfect, just enough to help with identification.) Then record what kind of birds they are, if you recognize them, how many birds you spotted, and what they were doing. If you don't recognize a bird and didn't get a picture of it, sketch out a quick drawing or make notes about its appearance, color, and size. You can then consult a field guide or photos online to try to identify it.

BIRD IDENTIFICATION

The closer you look at a bird, the more details you will see. The shape, color, size, and where you see it are important **field marks** that are necessary to tell the difference between, for instance, a House Finch and a Lesser Goldfinch. You might even write them down to remember when you look through a field guide book or website. For quick help, download the free **Cornell Merlin Bird ID app.** You enter when and where you saw the bird, the main color, size, and what the bird was doing, and get a gallery of possibilities. Or you can take a picture and let the app identify the bird. Click on your choice and get info like the bird call, fun facts, backyard tips, and the range of where it lives.

House Finch

DO A BACKYARD BIRD COUNT

Practice noting details about the birds at your feeder if you have one. Here are some important field marks to pay special attention to:

• Size (compared to a House Sparrow or pigeon)

• Main overall color of back, belly, wings

• Any bright colors on head, throat, belly, wings, tail.

• Any stripes on head, belly, throat.

• Behavior: spending time on the ground, in low bushes, middle of tree, top of tree, flying from perch to catch bugs.

• General location: desert, foothills, mountains, woods, riversides.

Cactus Wren

BIRD CALLS

You may hear a bird without seeing it; this will happen more than you'd think. If you recognize the call, mark it down and add it to your count. If you don't know the call (again, this will happen pretty often), use a bird ID smartphone app or head online to a website like All About Birds (www.allaboutbirds.org). Learn the calls of birds you recognize so you'll know them when you hear them, and check recordings of other birds common in your area.

RECORD YOUR FINDS

After you're done counting birds for 15 minutes, combine all of your finds into a list. Next, consider setting up an account on a citizen science site such as eBird. There, you can create a "life list" of species spotted over time, and you'll also contribute to science—the resulting maps help create a snapshot of birdlife over time.

THE CHRISTMAS BIRD COUNT

Once you get the hang of doing a bird count, consider participating in a national one. There are two long-running bird counts. One is the Christmas Bird Count, which has been around for 120 years. It takes place from mid-December to early January, and volunteers spread out to count birds in specific areas around each state and the country, with counts occurring in each local area for only one day. (So if you want to join in on the fun, tell your parents and prepare ahead of time!) To find out more, visit www.audubon.org /conservation/science/christmas-bird-count.

Mountain Chickadee

THE GREAT BACKYARD BIRD COUNT

This bird count is similar to the Christmas Bird Count, but it takes place everywhere, and you can participate if you spot birds for as little as 15 minutes, making it easy to join. It takes place in February. For more information and to sign up, visit www.birdcount.org

Keep track of the birds you see or spot here!

_____

_____

_____

_____

_____

_____

PLANT A HUMMINGBIRD, BEE & BUTTERFLY GARDEN

One way you can help wildlife wherever you live is by making your area a bit wilder. The easiest way to do that is to plant native plants. You don't need a huge amount of space to do this; even a small container garden with native plants can help attract—and feed—pollinators.

WHAT TO DO

Here are a few examples of how to attract some of the more sought-after pollinators:

• Common Sunflowers are easy to grow (sometimes they grow themselves when birds drop seeds). They produce a lot of pollen and nectar for butterflies and bees, and seeds for birds.

• Plant milkweed (Showy Milkweed or Narrow-leaf Milkweed). Monarch and Queen butterflies lay their eggs on milkweeds. You can spot the caterpillars munching away on the leaves if you take a close look.

• Plants with long tubular flowers, such as Hummingbird Trumpet, Autumn Sage, and Scarlet Bugler can all attract hummingbirds.

• Let the "weeds" be: Dandelions, purple asters, golden asters, spectacle pod mustards, and other flowers frequently volunteer (spring up without being planted by gardeners) in yards and gardens. They provide bees, butterflies, and other beneficial insects with pollen, nectar, and may be a host for caterpillars.

For a dedicated list, see this excellent write-up at the website for the Xerces Society: www.xerces.org/pollinator -conservation/pollinator-friendly-plant-lists.

(clockwise) Black-chinned Hummingbird, Common Buckeye, unidentified bumblebee species

Once you plant your hummingbird, bee, and butterfly garden, keep track of the insects and birds you spot here!

_____

_____

_____

_____

_____

SET UP A
WINDOW FEEDER

If you want to get an up-close look at birds, put up a window feeder. These transparent ledge-style feeders attach to a window via suction cups, and once the birds get used to the feeder and your presence on the other side of the glass, birds will chow down, enabling you to watch them from almost no distance at all.

BIRD NEST-CAMS

For a different kind of up-close look at birds, head online and look at the many different nest-cams offered on various bird sites. There are online nest-cams for eagles hawks, Ospreys, even hummingbirds.

For a list, visit www.allaboutbirds.org/cams.

MAKE YOUR WINDOWS SAFER FOR BIRDS

Hundreds of millions of birds are killed or injured each year when they accidentally fly into windows, often because they saw a reflection of nearby plants or the sky and thought it was a safe place to fly. Such collisions are often deadly, and they are a constant problem.

WHAT TO DO

There are a few simple safety steps you can take to help:

1. Close your blinds or curtains—this will make the window look more like a barrier. This is very important at night, when a lit-up room might seem like a welcoming place for a bird to fly.

2. When placing bird feeders, either keep them far away from windows (more than 20 feet) or keep them very close to windows—either directly on the window, via suction cups, or just a few feet away. (Even if a bird flies into a window from a close-by feeder, it won't fly fast enough to get seriously hurt.)

3. Consider purchasing "scare tape" or "flash tape"— reflective ribbons in iridescent colors that birds don't like— to help keep birds away from your windows.

4. Place ribbons, pinwheels, and other moving accessories in front of windows to scare birds away.

5. Keep plants away from windows, as birds often mistake them for part of the natural scenery outdoors.

WILDLIFE REHABILITATION NEAR YOU

If you see an animal get hurt or find one that you know is injured, keep your pets indoors, and then contact your local wildlife rehabilitation center or a permit-carrying wildlife rehabilitation expert. To find one, visit the California Department of Fish and Wildlife website.

WHAT TO DO

Baby birds often fall out of nests. If you find one that has only soft, downy feathers, put it back in the nest if you safely can. If its fully feathered, it's probably just spending a few days on the ground while it learns to fly. The parents are still feeding it, so do not pick it up or take it away. If it's in danger from a pet, in the hot sun, or where it might get hurt, try to hide it in a nearby bush where their parents can hear it calling. Otherwise, leave it alone or call a wildlife rehabilitator for help.

When baby birds get too big for the nest, their parents feed them on the ground until they can fly.

Have you ever encountered an injured animal? What happened to it? Were you able to help it? Write your story here.

_____

_____

_____

_____

_____

_____

_____

_____

_____

_____

_____

_____

_____

_____

_____

ASSEMBLING A COLLECTION OF STATE MINERALS & GEMS

Like state birds or flowers, most states have state gems and fossils, but you may have not heard or know about all of them. Still, state gems, minerals, and fossils are almost always selected for their long history in the state and for their beauty. Many were selected because school classes partitioned the state legislature to select a particular bird, insect, or rock. Best of all, many of these state gems, minerals, and fossils are easy to collect!

Note on Collecting Fossils: Fossils of **vertebrate animals** (any animal with a backbone) may not be collected on any federal or state lands except with permits issued to accredited institutions. Fossils include bones, teeth, skin impressions, footprints, tail drags, and other traces of activity of dinosaurs, fish, turtles, and mammals such as mammoths. **Invertebrate fossils** (animals that do not have a backbone, such as trilobites, ammonites, clams, snails, coral, shellfish, and insects) and **plant fossils** (such as petrified wood and leaf imprints) may be collected on public lands for personal use, but quantities are limited and restrictions or permits may be required by the various agencies. All collecting on personal property requires the owner's permission.

Collecting gems and minerals: Before you go out collecting, make sure that collecting is allowed where you're looking. (Do not go onto private property without permission when collecting, as that's illegal.) In many cases state parks and publicly owned land have sites where you can legally collect rocks, though it might take some homework first!

QUICK DEFINITION

A mineral usually consists of a combination of chemical elements. For example, table salt is a **mineral** (halite) made of two elements: sodium and chlorine. Sometimes, a single **chemical element** (like gold or silver) can be found in nature; those are considered minerals too. A **rock** is a combination of at least two minerals. A **fossil** is the preserved remains, remnant, imprint, or trace of an organism from a past geologic age, such as a bone, tooth, footprint, petrified wood, or leaf imprint.

GEM: BENITOITE

This beautiful, transparent, blue gemstone is an extremely rare form of barium titanium silicate crystal that resembles sapphire. The only gem-quality deposit occurs where it was first discovered. In 1907, a prospector found it near the San Benito River in San Benito County, hence its name. With a Mohs hardness of 6–6.5, it's hard enough to make into expensive jewelry. A commercial mine near Coalinga offers private gem hunts for individuals and families.

MINERAL: NATIVE GOLD

Since the discovery of gold in California in 1848, the state has been all about gold. The official nickname is "The Golden State," and the motto is "Eureka," which is Greek for "I have discovered it!" The official state gold rush ghost town, Bodie (near Yosemite National Park), once had a population of 10,000. Now it's a State Historic Park. In the first ten years after discovery, California prospectors mined 10 billion dollars worth of gold. You can still pan for gold in many tourist mining camps.

DINOSAUR: *AUGUSTYNOLOPHUS MORRISI*

This duck-billed dinosaur lived in what is now California from 60 to 70 million years ago. Only two specimens have ever been found, both near Fresno, California. The 10-foot-tall, 30-foot-long dinosaur was a plant eater with a mouth shaped like a duck's bill. You can see "Auggie" in the Dinosaur Hall of the Natural History Museum of Los Angeles County.

ASSEMBLING A COLLECTION OF STATE MINERALS & GEMS

ROCK: SERPENTINE

California's state rock is a little confusing. Technically speaking, serpentine isn't a rock at all: it's a group of minerals. The rock commonly referred to as serpentine contains two or more of those minerals. Serpentine sometimes gets a bad rap because it's related to materials known as asbestos, which were once widely used in fireproofing and industry. Scientists later learned that the minerals in that the minerals in asbestos can cause serious health problems.

But all that doesn't mean serpentine is dangerous; first, not all serpentine contains asbestos minerals, and even if you do, it can't hurt you unless you breathe in the rock's dust or fibers. That usually means either crushing the rock (common in mining), or finding a piece with very fine crystals.

Still, to be on the safe side, before collecting it, ask your parents, or pick up a polished piece of serpentine from a rock shop.

You can find serpentine in streambeds, and rocky hillsides and outcrops. The surface is usually shiny green with dark and light streaks like the skin of a serpent (snake), hence its name. Serpentine soil is high in metals and low in nutrition, which kills most plants. Only rugged plants especially adapted to the mineral composition can survive. With a Mohs hardness of 3-6, it's hard enough for gently worn jewelry, such as earrings, brooches, or pendants, and it is popular for rock sculptures and ornaments.

FOSSIL: SABER-TOOTHED CAT

About the size of a modern-day lion, these fearsome cats were widespread worldwide from 42 million years ago until the last species became extinct about 10,000 years ago. With powerful jaws and 8-inch-long upper canine teeth, the cats hunted giant ground sloths, rhinos, mammoths, and other large mammals of the era. They probably hunted in groups like lions today. Hundreds of cat bones were discovered in the La Brea Tar Pits in Los Angeles and can be seen at the museum located there, along with bones of hundreds of other animals that were trapped in the tar pits thousands of years ago.

GEOLOGY, GEMSTONES & FOSSILS CROSSWORD

ACROSS

3. The state dinosaur, *Augustynolophus morrisi*, had a mouth shaped like the bill of what kind of bird?

4. What name describes the kind of teeth that the state fossil cat had?

7. What is the most common color of serpentine?

Answers on page 129!

DOWN

1. What is the official state gold rush ghost town?

2. The mineral serpentine is named after what reptile?

5. What color is the gemstone Benitoite?

6. What kind of pits in Los Angeles trapped ancient animals thousands of years ago?

7. What precious metal does the state motto "Eureka" (I have found it!) refer to?

TESTING THE HARDNESS OF MINERALS

Hardness is a useful way to help identify your mineral finds. The **Mohs Hardness Scale**, on the right, ranks some common minerals in terms of hardness, or how easily they can be scratched. Talc, the lowest mineral on the scale, is so soft you can scratch it with your fingers. Diamond is famous for being one of the hardest minerals, and for good reason: almost no natural substances can scratch it.

Making your own hardness test kit is a good way to start learning hands-on with rocks and minerals. Determining a mineral's hardness is a good first step in trying to identify it.

The way the scale works is simple: any material lower on the scale can be scratched by materials above it. So gypsum can scratch talc, but talc can't scratch gypsum. Similarly, calcite, which is a 3, can scratch gypsum *and* talc.

WHAT YOU'LL NEED

Using the scale to test your finds usually goes like this: You find a mineral (not a rock!) and you're not sure what it is. You start out by trying to scratch it with your fingernail. If it leaves a scratch, then it's softer than 2.5 on the scale. Chances are, however, it won't leave a scratch. So you need to move up to a different piece of equipment with a known hardness.

Here are some common, easy-to-find examples:

- Fingernail: 2.5

- A real piece of copper (not a penny, as these coins aren't made of much copper anymore): 3

- Steel nail or a knife: 5.5–6 (for safety reasons, you should have an adult help you with these tests)

- A piece of quartz: 7

Talc
$Mg_3Si_4O_{10}(OH)_2$

Gypsum
$CaSO_4 \cdot 2H_2O$

Calcite
$CaCO_3$

Fluorite
CaF_2

Apatite
$Ca_5(PO_4)_3(F,Cl,OH)$

WHAT TO DO

To scratch it, you need to hold the to-be-scratched mineral firmly in one hand, and use a pointed area of the "scratching" mineral and press firmly, away from your body or fingers. If it leaves a scratch mark, it's softer than the "scratching" mineral. Obviously, for safety reasons you should make sure you have an adult conduct the actual scratch tests–don't handle a knife or a nail yourself.

Once you've found something that scratches it, you're pretty close to figuring out its hardness. Then it's just a matter of scratching it with other minerals from the chart or your scratching tools then seeing if you can figure out an even more specific range. Once you've narrowed down the hardness some more, looking up mineral hardness is easy online.

Note: You can also buy lab-calibrated "hardness pick" kits; these are much more accurate, but they can be expensive.

Keep track of your hardness tests here. Doing so can help you learn to identify your finds!

_____

_____

_____

_____

_____

_____

_____

_____

6

Orthoclase
$KAISi_3O_8$

7

Quartz
SiO_2

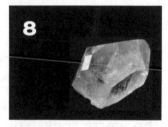

8

Topaz
$Al_2SiO_4(F,OH)_2$

9

Corundum
Al_2O_3

10

Diamond
C

LOOKING AT SOIL, DIRT, OR A DEAD LOG

Gems and colorful minerals are definitely showier than ordinary rocks, but sometimes if you get an up-close look, there may be more to see than just a rock, and the same is true for a dead log.

WHAT TO DO

A rock often creates its own micro-community of tiny insects, worms, and fungi. During the day it heats up in the sun, then as the night air cools, droplets of water condense on the warm rock. This moisture supports a tiny world of small creatures. Turn over a football-sized or smaller rock that is partially buried in the soil, and check the cluster of critters underneath. Be sure to put the rock back in its "nest" so the critters won't be disturbed too much.

A dead log might look, well, dead, but it's actually its own little universe. Insects, such as carpenter bees and beetles, burrow into the log to lay their eggs under the bark. Ants and beetles are busy tunneling or making a home (they often leave behind intricate patterns on the wood), and it's easy to spot tiny mushrooms and sometimes very colorful slime molds, which are food sources for other animals, such as slugs, snails, and insects. Once you start looking closely, it's easy to find a lot more like than you expected. Use a hand lens or magnifying glass to get a closer look.

Safety Note: If you have venomous spiders or snakes in your area, make sure you go out with an adult and take proper precautions (wear gloves, long pants, and so on) when digging in dirt or turning over logs.

WHAT YOU MIGHT SEE

• Slugs, pillbugs, or snails

• Lichen (an organism that consists of algae/bacteria and fungi, living together)

• Slime molds

• Spiders, ants, tiny insects, and other animals

QUICK QUESTION

Write down what critters you find in you quest to discover life hidden under rocks and logs.

_____

_____

_____

_____

_____

_____

MAKE A SUNPRINT

Nature is the most creative artist imaginable. Just look at the beautiful designs and patterns in flowers, leaves, ferns, grasses, weeds, and other natural objects. Using the power of the sun, special light-sensitive paper, and ordinary plants from your backyard, you can create beautiful prints of natural objects. You'll need flat objects that you can arrange on a sheet of blue sunprint paper. Here's how you make your masterpiece:

Note: Sunprint paper comes in various sizes and can be ordered inexpensively online.

WHAT TO DO

1. Gather flat natural objects, and think about how you will arrange them on a sheet of paper so their outlines will form an artistic image. The area that the plants block from the sun will turn out white on the print.

2. While indoors or in the shade, place your leaves and flowers, or whatever you gathered, on the sun paper. Place the sun paper on a table to keep it flat, or pin it to a piece of cardboard. If necessary, place a piece of clear plastic wrap over lightweight objects to hold them in place. The tighter the object is against the paper, the sharper the image will be.

3. Now place the arrangement in the direct sun and let it sit until the blue paper turns very pale blue, about two minutes.

4. Remove the objects and place the paper in a pan of plain water for about one minute. Watch the white image spring to life against the bright blue paper! Then repeat, one sunprint is never enough!

MAKE A PLANT PRESS

You'll probably want to make sunprints using flowers, some of the most beautiful objects in nature. But they will need to be flat to work on a sunprint. No problem. Botanists use plant presses to dry and preserve plants for study. You can get the same result with several large, heavy books and a stack of newspapers.

WHAT TO DO

- Use one book, or a hard tabletop or floor, as a firm bottom layer of the "press."

- Place 5–10 sheets of absorbent newspaper (not slick magazine paper) on the bottom, arrange the flower and leaves on a sheet of plain paper in a neat pattern, and then place 5–10 sheets of newspaper on top. You can stack several layers of plants plus newspaper on top of each other.

- Then stack heavy books on top to flatten the plant. Let the plants press for several days until all the moisture is absorbed by the newspaper.

- You can use the flattened plants for a sunprint, or glue an arrangement of plants to a sheet of paper to frame and hang on your wall.

MAKE A CAST OF AN ANIMAL TRACK

Learning to identify animal tracks is one of the easiest and most exciting ways to learn how to "read" who lives in the parks, trails, and natural areas close to your home or that you visit. From Coyotes to small kangaroo rats and lizards, they all leave tracks, and some track patterns even hint of mysteries that happened in the night. Learn what animals live in your area and make a collection of as many of their tracks as you can.

You might think that tracks won't last very long, but that is not always true, especially in damp soil. You can actually preserve a track using plaster. In loose sand, or if you don't have plaster handy, take a close-up photo instead. Field guides and online sources will help you identify the tracks that you find. Follow the instructions below to make your very own track cast collection. You can practice on your pet dog or cat, or on your own hand! Just fill a pie pan with wet plaster and make your handprint.

WHAT YOU WILL NEED

• Plaster of Paris powder

• A container and spoon for mixing

• Water

• A strip of plastic or cardboard that is larger than your track

• A paper clip

WHAT TO DO

1. Remove any twigs or leaves around the track.

2. Use the plastic or cardboard to create a "wall" around the track. Use the paper clip to secure the ends together. (On firm tracks, this may not be necessary.)

3. Add two parts plaster for every one part water (so if you use one cup of plaster, you should use a half cup of water).

4. Mix the plaster and water together until it is like pancake batter. Stir until the plaster isn't lumpy, usually at least a few minutes.

5. Pour the plaster inside your wall (but not directly onto the track), letting the plaster flow over the track gradually. Make sure you pour enough to cover the entire track to a depth of about $^3/_4$ inch.

6. Wait half an hour, then test the firmness of the plaster. Once it is hard enough, remove it by grabbing it at the edges. Wait a few days for it to dry completely.

Have an adult help you when creating a cast, as it can be a bit tricky. Once you have a cast, write on the back which animal it is and where you made it. You can even frame it.

BEAKS AND FEET

Tracks can tell you a lot about an animal. An animal's foot helps it catch food and escape enemies. A cat has soft paws that don't make noise when it stalks its prey, and claws and sharp teeth to catch and kill its food. Birds also have feet and bills designed for finding and eating their food. A hummingbird's bill is just the right size to probe a narrow flower for nectar. A duck's webbed feet help it paddle in water, and its flat bill makes it easy to strain mud for tiny insects. Look at these bird beaks and guess which birds they belong to.

1. I have a short, powerful bill for cracking seeds, like sunflowers.

2. I have a powerful, dagger-like bill for drilling holes in trees or the ground to look for insects.

3. I have a strong, curved bill perfect for scratching in leaves and dirt while looking for insects.

4. I have a long bill, long neck, and long legs for wading in water and catching fish.

5. I have a powerful hooked beak and strong feet for catching prey.

Answers on page 128!

Northern Flicker

Red-tailed Hawk

Great Blue Heron

House Finch

Curve-billed Thrasher

MAKE A SELF-PORTRAIT USING NATURE

WHAT YOU WILL NEED

• Several blank pieces of paper

• A glue stick, if you want to create a permanent piece of art

WHAT TO DO

With an adult, start out by gathering some twigs; these are a great way to create a general outline of your face. Then start thinking about the color of your skin, hair, and eyes, and look around for natural objects that are a close match. It's best to choose from things that you know are safe to touch: rocks and pebbles, sand, dandelions, flower petals, oak and maple leaves, grass, moss, tree bark, and so on. If you're not sure if you can touch it, leave it be, or ask an adult. That way, you can avoid Poison Ivy, Poison Oak, Poison Sumac, and anything icky.

When you're done, take a picture of your portrait, and then put your natural parts back where you found them, and your paper in the recycling or trash. Alternately, you can glue each object to the paper and then frame it. Just make sure no little kids have access to the actual leaves and flowers and such. Throw away any leftovers in the garbage.

LEARNING TO IDENTIFY BASIC GROUPS OF BUGS

If you want to learn about insects, start by learning to identify the basic groups (or orders) of insects. Some, such as butterflies and moths, you might already know, but there are quite a few more to discover. This list isn't all-inclusive, but it gives you a fun idea of some of the insects you can find!

BUTTERFLIES & MOTHS (LEPIDOPTERA)

White-Lined Sphinx Moth

Monarch

Two-tailed Swallowtail

Southern Dogface

Painted Lady

Great Blue Hairstreak

ANTS, BEES & WASPS (HYMENOPTERA)

Honeybee

Bumblebee

Carpenter Bee

Native bees

FLIES (DIPTERA)

House Fly

Hover Fly

Flower Fly

Bee Fly

Red Tachinid Fly

LEARNING TO IDENTIFY
BASIC GROUPS OF BUGS

BEETLES (COLEOPTERA)

Lady Bug

Goldenrod
Soldier Beetle

Black and Red
Blister Beetle

Longhorn Beetle

TRUE BUGS (HEMIPTERA)

Assassin Bug

Cicada

Leafhopper

Stinkbug

Treehopper

Aphids

SPIDERS (ARANEAE)

Black Widow

Tarantula

Crab Spider

Wolf Spider

GRASSHOPPERS, CRICKETS (ORTHOPTERA)

Grasshopper

Cricket

COCKROACHES, TERMITES (BLATTODEA)

Cockroach

Termite

DAMSELFLIES & DRAGONFLIES (ODONATA)

Dragonflies

MANTIS (MANTODEA)

Praying Mantis

LEARNING TO IDENTIFY BASIC GROUPS OF BUGS

NON-INSECTS

A venomous
Desert Centipede

Millipede

Scorpion

Isopod, pillbug

Dog Tick

QUICK QUIZ

Which bugs can cause painful bites or stings if you pick one up?

A. Spiders

B. Ticks

C. Centipedes

D. Scorpions

E. Bees

F. All of them

Answer on page 128!

MAKE YOUR YARD A LITTLE WILDER

Many insect populations are at risk. Habitat destruction, insecticide spraying (which kills a lot more than just mosquitoes), and water pollution can all play a role. Lawns, in particular, are part of the problem, as they are incredibly widespread, and not all that useful for many plants and animals. That's why it's helpful to make your yard a bit wilder.

WHAT TO DO

With your parents' OK, make a portion of your yard a little bit more like nature. Plant a mix of native flowering plants there, don't spray pesticides or herbicides in that area or mow it as heavily, and leave out some deadwood for insect habitat. Then, over time, keep track of the critters you find, and compare it to the rest of your yard. You'll find that even a small patch of plants can attract critters you may have never seen before.

Before you create a "wild patch" in your yard, write down your plan below. What are you hoping to attract?

_____

_____

_____

_____

RAISE NATIVE CATERPILLARS & RELEASE THEM

Finding a caterpillar is one of the highlights of spring and summer. But unless it's a really well-known caterpillar, like a Monarch, identifying caterpillars can be tricky for beginners. Many caterpillars, including all of the classic "inchworms," will actually end up being moths. Even the name scientists use for these moths—Geometridae—is a reference to geometry and how these caterpillars "measure" as they walk.

But you don't need to identify your caterpillar to rear it; after all, one of the most fun ways to identify a moth or a butterfly is after it's turned into an adult!

WHAT YOU'LL NEED

• A butterfly house (it's best to purchase a high-quality one online first)

• An ample supply of fresh leaves

• A water source for the leaves, but one that the caterpillar can't enter (pill bottles work great)

WHAT TO DO

When you find a caterpillar, immediately note what plant you find it on or, if it's on the ground, the plants that are nearby. These are likely the caterpillar's host plants (the ones it needs to eat to become an adult). If you're unsure of which plants to gather, bring in a sampling of several different kinds. If you want an exact answer, post a photo of your caterpillar on a site like BugGuide.net and ask for help on finding out what it eats. If you think you might know the species, check out the website butterfliesandmoths.org. It has a lot of info and photos of caterpillars and adults.

Once you have the caterpillar and the host plants, you'll need to ready your butterfly

Owlet Moth caterpillar

Butterfly and moth metamorphosis has four stages: egg, caterpillar, pupa, adult.

house. Many common commercially available houses are mesh cylinders.

First, you need to prepare your water source for the host plants. **Do not** provide a water dish or another water source at the bottom of a butterfly house; caterpillars drown easily. Instead, have a parent help you drill or cut a hole in a small container like an old pill bottle, and put the plant stems into the water source (but make sure the caterpillar can't fall into the water and drown).

Over time, you'll need to replace the leaves, and clean up its poop (known as frass). Eventually, the caterpillar will begin to pupate. This fascinating process is called **metamorphosis**, and all butterflies, moths, and even bees do it. When the caterpillar makes its cocoon, it's whole body turns to mush, then reforms as a completely different creature. Watching a worm-like creature turn into a beautiful butterfly is like watching a mysterious magic act.

Many butterflies lay their eggs on a wide range of plants, but some are specialists. If you want to find Monarch and Queen Butterfly caterpillars, plant or find wild milkweed plants. Black Swallowtail Butterflies lay their eggs on dill and fennel, popular plants for herb gardens.

Five-spotted Hawkmoth caterpillar

Of course, things can go wrong when collecting wild caterpillars: parasitic wasps often attack or infest caterpillars; if your cage is dirty, they can get sick; and if you find a caterpillar in late summer, it might be one that overwinters as a pupa. Still, with practice, there's a good chance that you'll get to watch moths and butterflies all summer long if you work at it hard enough!

GET TO KNOW CALIFORNIA'S NATIVE BEES

If you've been following the news, you know that bee populations are in trouble. But you're probably most familiar with honeybees, which are actually an introduced species native to Europe, not the US. Think of honeybees as farm animals. The honeybees you see in your yard? In a sense, those are kind of like escaped chickens or cows.

Domesticated honeybee populations have run into trouble over the past few decades due to a combination of factors, including pests (especially the Varroa mite), pesticide use, and habitat loss. These domesticated insects play a critical role in pollinating agricultural crops, especially almonds, blueberries, and cherries.

Honeybees aren't the only bees in the US that are threatened, however. Honeybees get much of the press, but thousands of native bee species live in the US and many are threatened due to loss of habitat, destruction of native wildflowers (their

QUICK QUIZ

Which one of these is a Bee?

A.   B.   C.

Answers on page 128!

food), and loss of suitable nesting sites. They range from the familiar bumblebees that buzz around your flowers to carpenter bees which bore into wood. Bees, flies, and beetles are common flower pollinators. Note that bees have long antennas, while flies have short, stubby antennas.

BEES

Bumblebee

Cactus Bees

Carpenter Bee

Sweat Bee

Mining Bee

Mason Bee

BEE LOOK-ALIKES & BEETLES

Flower Fly

Syrphid Fly

Red Longhorn Beetle

START AN INSECT COLLECTION

If you love bugs, creating a bug collection can help you observe them up close, but if you're not into killing bugs, there's another option. When you're out in nature, chances are you'll notice dead insects if you're paying attention. If a bug is dead but in reasonably good shape, you can add it to your collection. You'll be surprised at what you find: butterflies and moths, gorgeous beetles, and so on (after all, insects don't live very long).

One of the easiest ways to store insects is with a Riker Mount, an inexpensive glass case with padding that holds the insects against the glass. Or you can buy a shadowbox display case or picture frame (deep enough so the glass top doesn't touch the back) and line it with cardboard and fabric to pin the insects into.

OPTIONAL PROJECT

If you want to collect live samples, placing them in a zip-top plastic bag and freezing them is one way to kill them humanely. On sites like BugGuide.net, you can also look up "killing jars" online that use common household chemicals.

What is your favorite type of insect? Why?

_____

_____

_____

_____

89

MAKE AN ULTRAVIOLET BUG TRAP

WHAT YOU'LL NEED

- A light—either a normal lantern or a UV lamp (simple blacklights available online work)

- An extension cord

- An old bedsheet or a curtain (a light-colored one is best)

- Two sections of rope

- A pair of scissors

- Flashlights

- A camera

WHAT TO DO

With an adult supervising, cut holes in the corners at one end of the bedsheet, and have the adult help you tie a section of rope to each hole in the bedsheet or curtain. (Curtains often have ready-made loops that make things easier.)

Then look for a good spot to find bugs; generally, the wilder it is, the better, but you'll need to be within reach of an outdoor-safe extension cord so you can plug in your light. Near woods, bushes, or other plants is good, but even the middle of a suburban yard will have all sorts of bugs you've likely never seen.

Tie one rope to a tree branch, a bird feeder hook, or another support, and then pull the rope on the other side of the curtain until the whole thing is taut, hanging like a movie screen. Tie that rope to a chair or anything else

White-lined Sphinx Moth

heavy enough to hold it. About an hour before sundown, find a chair and place it on either side of the curtain, set your light on it, and plug the into the extension cord, shining it onto the curtain (but not close enough to touch it).

Then wait and make periodic visits to the sheet to see what you find! Heading out with a flashlight in one hand and a camera in another is an easy way to record your finds (and identify them later on). On a nightly basis, you can look on the wall around outside porch lights to see moths and beetles attracted to the light.

Once you get a look at the insects you've attracted, wait a while longer and visit again later in the night (some of the best bug hunting is late at night).

Note: When you are observing moths, the light might shine on you and your clothes a bit, so it's possible (though not all that likely) to have moths or other bugs land on you. To avoid this, wear a dark shirt (not one that matches the "moth sheet"). A few bugs may land on you, but gently brushing them off with a stick or a gloved hand is enough to make them fly away.

Rustic Sphinx Moth

Ten-lined June Beetle

CRICKET MATH

Crickets are famously noisy insects; the males rub their front wings (not their legs!) together to attract females. That much, you probably knew. But did you know that you can count a cricket's chirps to tell the approximate temperature outside?

The math is simple: Go outside and listen for a cricket that's chirping. Count the number of its chirps for 13 seconds, then add 40 to that total. Then check it against the temperature for your area: go to www.noaa.gov and find your local weather in the top-right corner.

Pretty wild, right? Try it again on a different day and record your findings below.

The reason this works out is actually relatively simple: Crickets, like all insects, are cold-blooded, so their body temperature depends on the surrounding air. So when it's warmer, their metabolism speeds up, and so do the chirps! When it's colder, their chirps slow down.

Number of chirps in 13 seconds _____ + 40 = _____

Number of chirps in 13 seconds _____ + 40 = _____

Number of chirps in 13 seconds _____ + 40 = _____

Number of chirps in 13 seconds _____ + 40 = _____

Number of chirps in 13 seconds _____ + 40 = _____

Number of chirps in 13 seconds _____ + 40 = _____

[1] Original research via Dr. Peggy LeMone and James Larsen. https://www.questia.com/library/journal/1G1-272666064/the-sound-of-crickets-using-evidence-based-reasoning

BUGS & INSECTS CROSSWORD

ACROSS

2. These beautiful fast-flying insects zoom through the summer air, snatching bugs in midair.

3. This insect is very important for many farmers, as it helps pollinate their crops, but it's not native to North America.

4. These hopping insects have powerful hind legs, but they also are excellent flyers if you try to catch one.

7. Ladybugs are this kind of insect.

8. This insect is famous for chirping at night, and if you count its chirps over thirteen seconds, you can even use it as a thermometer!

DOWN

1. The word for a larval (juvenile) butterfly.

5. These critters aren't insects because they have eight instead of six legs. Some are **venomous**, and large, hairy ones can be a little scary looking.

6. Butterflies usually fly during the day; this group of related insects look similar, but most (but not all) fly at night.

Answers on page 129!

START LOOKING AT MUSHROOMS

You've probably seen mushrooms, a type of fungus, in the grocery stores or growing in parks or woodlands. Mushrooms are widespread in deserts, chaparral, grasslands, and foothills, but are most common on riversides and in damp mountain forests. California has thousands of species, and scientists think millions more exist around the world.

Many fungi have a **mutualistic** (equally helpful) relationship with trees, bushes, and wildflowers that helps both of them get nutrients. Tiny, thread-like filaments called mycelia (much like roots) of the fungi grow into the plant roots and live off the sugars the plant produces. In turn the mycelia carry large amounts of nutrients and water from the soil to the plant roots.

Other fungi are **saprobes** (they consume dead or dying trees or other natural materials). This returns the nutrients in the leaves and wood back into the soil to be used again. Still others are microscopic but very important, such as the yeast that helps make the bread for your peanut butter and jelly sandwich, or the mold that grows in fuzzy, purple splotches on old bread.

The fungus mycelia live underground until it sends up a stem with a mushroom, the fruiting body (like an apple) that produces spores (like the seeds in an apple). In California, mushrooms can be classified in a few simple ways. Obviously, this list is not all-inclusive, and it is no replacement for a field guide (or five!), but these general categories are helpful to know.

Important Note: Do not eat wild mushrooms. Some are very toxic (poisonous) to eat and tricky to identify. Wait until you're older and have trained, experienced adults to help you out.

CAP & STEM WITH GILLS

Mushrooms with a stem and a cap, with gills underneath.

Red Fly Agaric

Milk Mushroom

Inky Cap
Mushroom

Russula

Green-gilled
Parasol

CAP & STEM WITH PORES

Mushrooms with a cap and a stem, but with tiny holes
(pores) underneath.

King Bolete

START LOOKING AT MUSHROOMS

SHELF MUSHROOMS

Mushrooms that mostly grow out from trees, like a shelf, or a bracket; they can have either pores or gills.

Oyster Mushroom

Artist's Conk

Turkey Tail

ROUND MUSHROOMS THAT DON'T OPEN

Mushrooms that grow in a ball or oval shape, with or without a stalk. Most puffballs are golf-ball sized, but some can be as large as a soccer ball. Step on one and it sends out a puff of powdery spores. But be careful, spores aren't healthy to breathe.

Desert Shaggy Mane

Earth Star

Puffball

Puffball releasing spores

SURPRISING MUSHROOMS

Mushrooms that are hard to describe because of their bizarre shapes or weird consistency.

Coral Fungi   Morels   False Morels

TIPS FOR SPOTTING MUSHROOMS

- Look for mushrooms after a rain (they can pop up quite quickly).

- Look near the bases of dying trees or on dead logs.

- Mushrooms often seem to grow from the ground, but they might actually be growing from wood in the soil.

- Slime molds often grow under bark.

START LOOKING AT MUSHROOMS

SLIME MOLDS

Slime molds were once considered fungi, but they're now classified differently. Still, they are often grouped together with fungi, so here are a few! They're really weird, and by the way, they can move—but slowly, so you need a time-lapse camera to see it. You gotta love their common names!

Dog Vomit
Slime Mold

Chocolate Tube
Slime Mold

Wolf's Milk
Slime Mold

1. Page through a field guide to mushrooms, then go and look for them in your area, especially if it has rained lately (mushrooms often spring up after rains). Jot down notes about them here! But remember: **Don't eat wild mushrooms.** Take notes and pictures instead!

_____

_____

_____

_____

_____

2. Sketch your mushroom finds here!

MAKE MUSHROOM SPORE PRINTS

Mushrooms reproduce via spores. Spores are too small to see individually without a microscope, but there's an easy and fun way to spot them: by making a spore print. For a number of technical reasons, spores aren't considered the same thing as a seed in a plant, but the basic idea is the same: spores help fungi reproduce. And they do that by leaving microscopic spores behind almost everywhere. Spore colors vary by species, and they can produce some neat results. To see for yourself, make a spore print.

WHAT YOU'LL NEED

• Small bowls or cups

• White paper and, if possible, some construction paper of various colors

• Different kinds of mushrooms, with caps and pores, or caps and gills

WHAT TO DO

With a knife, cut off the cap of each mushroom—or take a good section of a shelf mushroom—and place it on top of a piece of paper. (The gills or pores should be facing down onto the paper.) Place a small bowl or a cup over each mushroom. Mushroom spore colors vary a lot, so it's helpful to change up the paper color; a mushroom with light-colored spores won't show up well on white paper, for instance. Wait an hour or so, remove the bowl, and throw the mushroom in the trash. Then admire the spore print left behind!

Important Note: Have an adult handle the knife, and don't make spore prints in your kitchen or another area where food is served, or where someone could mistake the mushrooms for food. A garage is a good place to make spore prints.

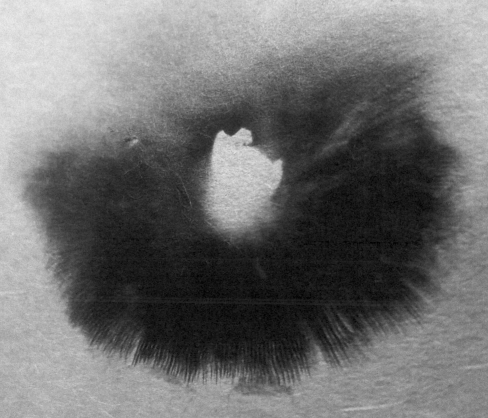

CARVE ARTIST'S CONK

Artist's Conk is a special kind of shelf mushroom that grows on dead or dying trees. At first glance, it doesn't look like much. It's pretty plain looking on the top—oval shaped and brown and white—and underneath it's just a drab white.

Artist's Conk gets its name because its white pores turn a dark brown when scratched. And the scratches then stay that way, making it a favorite of "scratch artists." This makes Artist's Conk something like nature's Etch A Sketch.

Of course, to identify Artist's Conk, you'll need an adult's help and a field guide (see page 122), but it's not too tricky to spot once you start looking.

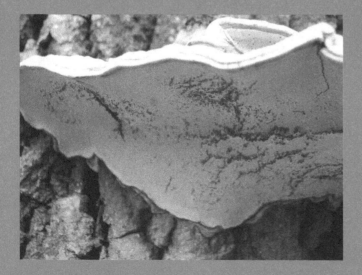

Before you carve your Artist's Conk, you might want to practice writing down your message here. When you're writing on a mushroom, you can't use an eraser, so practicing here first can help you get it right.

_____

_____

_____

_____

_____

_____

_____

_____

_____

_____

_____

_____

_____

SPOTTING THE MOON, PLANETS, MILKY WAY & ORION

Winter, when the nights are clear, is one of the best seasons for stargazing. There aren't any bugs, and you don't have to stay up late for it to get really dark. Also, some of the best constellations are visible during the winter. So if you dress warmly, grab a lawn chair, and find a small telescope or binoculars, you can see the planets, the moon, even the **Orion constellation** and the **Pleiades.** If you can find a really dark place without any city lights, you might even be able to see the **Milky Way.** It's a bright streak of stars that arcs across the night sky from north to south.

WHAT YOU WILL NEED

• Warm clothes

• A lawn chair

• A small telescope or, if you don't have one, binoculars

• A field guide and/or virtual planetarium software like Stellarium (which is free for Windows computers and Macs)

WHAT TO DO

First, figure out what you want to see before you head out. That's where a good field guide comes in. Virtual planetarium software is great too, because it can show you exactly what the sky will look like wherever you are (and whenever you want).

Starting with the moon is always a good idea, as it's bright and impossible to miss when it's up. The best time to observe the moon is in the "first quarter" when only one-half of the moon is lit up, as it reveals a lot more detail than a full moon, when all that reflected sunlight washes out the view. If you have a small telescope, try holding a smartphone over the eyepiece, and see if you can snap some pictures. This can be tricky, but if you take a bunch of pictures and fiddle with the settings, you can get some wonderful shots (there are also phone mounts you can buy fairly inexpensively online, though you have to get the right model for your phone).

The Pleiades star cluster, or Seven Sisters, is about 400 million light years from Earth (NASA Hubble Space Telescope).

After you take a look at the moon, make sure you get a chance to see Jupiter, Saturn, Mars, and Venus. You'll need to refer to your field guide or planetarium software for when and where to look for each, because they appear to move through the sky over time. Still, it's worth the effort: seeing Saturn's rings for the first time will make you gasp.

Note: Don't expect to see the rings like you would in a picture from NASA—the planets will look pretty darn small. But if you're patient and you focus just right, you'll see the planets for real. It's an amazing experience. Even if you just have binoculars, you can often spot Jupiter's largest moons: Io, Europa, Ganymede, and Callisto.

Finally, even if you only have a small telescope or binoculars, make sure to take a look at the constellation Orion. Easy to spot throughout much of the late fall and winter, it's famous for Orion's Belt, a line of three evenly spaced stars at the center of the constellation. If you look just below the belt, you'll see a star that looks a bit smudged; it's actually not a star at all. It's a **nebula**, an area where stars are forming. Viewed through binoculars or a small telescope, it's a wonderful sight. The same is true for the Pleiades, a bright star cluster with seven stars, also known as the Seven Sisters. To find them, simply follow from Orion's Belt up and to the right. If you're just looking with your eyes, it looks like a little smudge, but through binoculars or a telescope, it looks kind of like a miniature version of the Big Dipper.

Milky Way over Mount Whitney, California

SPOT THE INTERNATIONAL SPACE STATION (ISS)

If you really want an amazing sight, see if you can observe the International Space Station as it passes overhead. Continuously inhabited by astronauts since the year 2000, the International Space Station is massive—longer than a football field—and its huge solar panels reflect a lot of light back to Earth. This makes it incredibly bright in the night sky as it passes overhead.

WHAT TO DO

To spot it, visit the excellent website Spot the Station (spotthestation.nasa.gov), and check the forecast for the next times the station will pass overhead at your location. It'll be visible either in the morning (sometimes quite early) or in the evening. But, if you are patient, there are quite a few options, and you can make observing the ISS a fun habit. If you want a challenge, try snapping a photo of it as it passes overhead.

And once you spot it, you can visit the website www.howmany peopleareinspacerightnow.com to learn who was aboard the ISS as it flew by.

1. What was it like seeing the International Space Station?

_____

_____

2. How long did you see it, and how bright was it in the sky compared to the stars and planets?

_____

_____

International
Space Station

CONDUCT A BACKYARD
BIO-BLITZ

A **bio-blitz** is an event where nature lovers—usually in a large group—try to record all of the life in a given area during a set period of time. For scientists and nature lovers, bio-blitzes help provide a snapshot of an area's **biodiversity** (everything alive) at any one time. Every spring in April, many cities compete in an nationwide bio-blitz City Challenge with lots of volunteers of all ages going out to see which city can record the most plant and animal species. To participate, see https://citynaturechallenge.org.

You don't need to be a scientist to do a bio-blitz; you can do one yourself or with your friends. And you can do one wherever you are: in your backyard, on a trip, even from the window of a car or from an apartment balcony. The basic idea is simple: You want to try to identify as many life-forms as you can within a certain amount of time.

WHAT YOU WILL NEED

• A magnifying glass

• A smartphone

• A notebook and pen for each person

• Field guides

WHAT TO DO

The simplest way to start off is in your backyard or a green space near to where you live. Have an adult set a timer for 15 minutes or half an hour. Start out with the easy stuff first: the grass, any weeds that you recognize (dandelions), and birds or mammals (such as chipmunks or squirrels). It's helpful to be systematic (start in one area, and look it over carefully) before moving on to the next.

For each thing, write down what you think it is, and where you found it. Take a picture or draw it if you don't know what it is and want to look it up. In official bio-blitzes, each volunteer has a form with blanks to list specific location, time, and so on, but the form below (which you can copy into your notebook) should work for yours. See how many different kinds of animals and plants you can find!

Bonus: If you can look it up, try to find the **scientific name** for what you found. Scientific names exist to make it easier for scientists to talk to each other clearly. For example, there are three main different kinds of bears in North America: black bears, brown bears, and polar bears. So the word "bear" isn't very specific. And for many creatures, including insects, there simply aren't any common names. A scientific name is a special name that has two parts: a **genus name**, which is like a person's last name, and is shared with other related animals, and a **species name**, which is like your first name. Together, that name is unique for that plant or animal. For example, only one plant has the name *Taraxacum officinale*: the Common Dandelion, and scientists all over the world can refer to it, even if they don't speak the same language!

Note: If you're doing this from a car window on a long drive, you obviously won't be able to take photos. However, you can still note the birds, trees, roadside plants and such that you see, and any deer, foxes, Coyotes, or other critters along the way.

WHAT IS IT?	LOCATION	SCIENTIFIC NAME
Plants		
Common Dandelion	By the swing set	*Taraxacum officinale*
Coast Live Oak	In the front yard	*Quercus agrifolia*
Birds		
House Finch	On the oak tree	*Haemorhous mexicanus*
Mammals		
Desert Cottontail	Under bush	*Sylvilagus audubonii*
Insects		
Monarch Butterfly	On yellow flower	*Danaus plexippus*

CONTRIBUTE TO A COMMUNITY SCIENCE PROJECT

If your parents have a smartphone, or you have one of your own, ask if it's OK to download **iNaturalist.** This app is all about nature. It's a wonderful way to keep track of and identify your finds, and you can help science in the process.

WHAT TO DO

The way it works is simple. You sign up (you have to be 13 years old to have your own account), and then you take a photo of an animal, plant, or mushroom that you spot. You then create an observation, add the photo, and click on the "What Did You See?" button. The app will run the photo through a computer program that will attempt to identify it; the program isn't perfect, but it often helps you narrow down what you found.

Then, if you share the observation and location online, other observers (including experts) can help confirm your identification (or propose a new one). Once an observation has two identifications that are the same, it's considered "research grade," and it can be used by scientists! In fact, this might happen faster than you think.

Note: If you or your parents are concerned about your privacy (ask them if you're not sure), you don't have to post your exact location—there's an option to click "Obscured" under "Geolocation." This will keep people from seeing exactly where you made your observation and instead only gives a large range instead.

Keep track of your community science discoveries here by making a "life list" of the plants, animals, and fungi you've spotted.

_____

_____

_____

_____

_____

_____

_____

_____

_____

_____

_____

_____

_____

NATURE BINGO

Circle the nature you see, and see who gets a bingo first!

NATURE

BINGO

YELLOW FLOWER	BEE	MAMMAL	BIRD HOPPING ON GROUND	GRASS
CONIFEROUS TREE (EVERGREEN)	ROCK	RED FLOWER	FRUIT	CLOUD
SPIDER	ANT	FREE THE SKY SPACE	BEETLE	OAK TREE
THE MOON	SEED	BIRD IN TREE	BUSH	STAR (THE SUN COUNTS)
CACTUS	WHITE FLOWER	PINE CONE	BUTTERFLY	BIRD FLYING

NATURE

BINGO

RED FLOWER	BEE	MAMMAL	SEED	OAK TREE
ANT	BIRD IN TREE	WHITE FLOWER	CONIFEROUS TREE (EVERGREEN)	SPIDER
ROCK	FRUIT	FREE SPACE THE SKY	PINE CONE	BEETLE
THE MOON	BIRD ON GROUND	GRASS	STAR (THE SUN COUNTS)	BIRD FLYING
BUTTERFLY	BUSH	MUSHROOM	CLOUD	YELLOW FLOWER

RECORD YOUR ACTIVITIES, DISCOVERIES & FINDS HERE

If you find something neat, make a sketch to the right to help you remember details so you can compare your drawing to a field guide or another reference later.

_____

_____

_____

_____

_____

_____

_____

_____

_____

_____

_____

_____

_____

_____

RECORD YOUR ACTIVITIES, DISCOVERIES & FINDS HERE

If you find something neat, make a sketch to the right to help you remember details so you can compare your drawing to a field guide or another reference later.

_____

_____

_____

_____

_____

_____

_____

_____

_____

_____

_____

_____

_____

_____

RECORD YOUR ACTIVITIES, DISCOVERIES & FINDS HERE

If you find something neat, make a sketch to the right to help you remember details so you can compare your drawing to a field guide or another reference later.

_____

_____

_____

_____

_____

_____

_____

_____

_____

_____

_____

_____

_____

RECORD YOUR ACTIVITIES, DISCOVERIES & FINDS HERE

If you find something neat, make a sketch to the right to help you remember details so you can compare your drawing to a field guide or another reference later.

_____

_____

_____

_____

_____

_____

_____

_____

_____

_____

_____

_____

_____

_____

RECOMMENDED READING

Acorn, John. *Bugs of Northern California*. Lone Pine, 2002. (Children's book)

Daniels, Jaret C. *Backyard Bugs: An Identification Guide to Common Insects, Spiders, and More*. Cambridge, Minnesota: Adventure Publications, 2017.

Eisner, Thomas. *For Love of Insects*. Cambridge, Mass: Belknap Press of Harvard University Press, 2003.

Himmelman, John. *Discovering Moths: Nighttime Jewels in Your Own Backyard*. Camden, Maine: Down East Books, 2002.

Johnson, Jinny. *Animal Tracks and Signs*. Chartwell Books, Inc. 2011. Print. (Age 10 and up).

Lynch, Dan R. *Fossils for Kids: An Introduction to Paleontology*. Cambridge, Minnesota: Adventure Publications, 2020.

Lynch, Dan R. *Rock Collecting for Kids: An Introduction to Geology*. Cambridge, Minnesota: Adventure Publications, 2018.

Miller, George. *Wildflowers of Southern California*. Cambridge, Minnesota: Adventure Publications, 2017. Print.

Miller, George. *Wildflowers of Northern California*. Cambridge, Minnesota: Adventure Publications, 2018. Print.

Miller, George. *Wildflowers of Arizona & New Mexico*. Cambridge, Minnesota: Adventure Publications, 2020. Print.

Miller, George. *Native Plant Gardening for Birds, Bees & Butterflies: Southern California*. Cambridge, Minnesota: Adventure Publications, 2021. Print.

Miller, George. *Wildflowers of New Mexico*. www.WildflowersNM.com. Online.

Poppele, Jonathan. *Night Sky: A Field Guide to the Constellations*. Cambridge, Minnesota: Adventure Publications, 2009. Print.

Tekiela, Stan. B*irding for Beginners: California: Your Guide to Feeders, Food, and the Most Common Backyard Birds* (Bird-Watching Basics). Cambridge, Minnesota: Adventure Publications, 2020. Print.

Tekiela, Stan. *Birds of California Field Guide* (Bird Identification Guides). Cambridge, Minnesota: Adventure Publications, 2021. Print.

GLOSSARY

Adaptations The features of a plant or animal that help it thrive where it lives from generation to generation.

Bio-blitz An organized count of plants and animals carried on for a set time period in a specific place.

Biome A community of animals and plants that live in a specific kind of climate and environment.

Biodiversity The number of different kinds, or species, of living things that live in an area.

Chemical element One of the 92 naturally occurring chemicals such as oxygen, carbon, etc., that make up all matter on Earth.

Commodities Farm products such as cattle, corn, and soybeans that are sold worldwide.

Conifer A tree that produces seeds in cones, such as pine, fir, and spruce trees.

Deciduous A tree or shrub that loses its leaves in the winter.

Dormant A sleep-like state when a plant or animal is not active.

Drought deciduous A plant that loses its leaves during dry conditions or during droughts.

Equator The midpoint on the earth's surface between the North and South Poles; the days and nights are always equal in length, and the latitude measurement is 0.

Estuaries The marshy area where a river flows into the ocean.

Evergreen A tree or shrub that doesn't lose its leaves and stays green all winter.

Extinction When all members of a plant or animal species are gone forever.

Extirpated Animals and plants that have been wiped out from their original habitat but may still live elsewhere.

Field Marks The size and colors of a bird that help identify it.

GLOSSARY

Fossil The preserved remains, remnant, imprint, or trace of a plant or animal from a past geologic age, such as a bone, tooth, footprint, petrified wood, or leaf imprint.

Genus name All living thing have a unique scientific name made up of two parts a genus, which is like an organism's last name, and which it shares with other related organisms, and its species name, which is like its first name. See *Scientific Name.*

Germinate When a seed sprouts and begins to grow.

Intertidal Zone The coastal area where tides wash in and out.

Introduced An animal or plant that was brought to an area (example: cows in the US).

Invasive An introduced species that outcompetes native plants and animals, harming the ecosystem.

Invertebrate animals All animals that do not have a backbone. For instance snails, clams, butterflies, beetles, ants.

Keystone species A plant or animal that many other plants and animals depend on to survive.

Killing frost When temperatures reach about 28° F., cold enough to freeze the water in most plants and kill them.

Latitude How far north or south a person or place is from the equator; the equator is at a latitude of 0; the North Pole is 90 degrees north.

Mediterranean climate A specific type of climate with dry summers and cool, wet winters.

Metamorphosis The process butterflies, moths, and bees pass through to change from larvae (caterpillars) to adults that can fly.

Milky Way Earth's home galaxy; all the stars you see in the sky are part of the Milky Way; the galaxy get its name for the milky band of light often visible that is caused by light reflecting off the dust in between the galaxy's stars

Mineral A chemical combination of two or more elements; individual elements (copper, gold) are considered minerals as well.

Mohs Hardness Scale The relative scale of mineral hardness, from the softest, talc (1), to the hardest, diamond (10).

Mutalistic A relationship between two organisms where each one gets something of value/or benefit.

Mycelia The thread-like filaments of fungi that connect to the roots of plants.

Native An animal, plant or organism found naturally in an area.

Nebula An enormous gas and dust cloud between stars where stars are born.

Nonnative An animal, plant, or organism not naturally found in an area; note that not all nonnative animals are invasive.

Northern Hemisphere The part of the Earth north of the equator.

Orion (constellation) A group of stars named for a hunter in ancient Greek mythology.

Pacific Flyway The route between the Rocky Mountains and the Pacific coastline that takes migrating birds from Canada to South America.

Pelagic Zone The open ocean with deep water.

Phenology The study of how the seasons and other natural cycles effect plants and animals over time.

Pleiades A cluster of seven dim stars barely visible with the unaided eye.

Predators Animals that eat other animals.

Rain shadow A region that receives little rainfall because a mountain range blocks the flow of moisture from the ocean. Death Valley is in the rain shadow of the Sierra Nevada range.

Rock A combination of two or more minerals.

GLOSSARY

Saprobes Mushrooms that feed on dead or dying material (often wood or plant parts).

Scientific name Because there are so many different plants and animals and other lifeforms, scientists give every organism a unique name, usually derived from Latin/Greek. This scientific name has two parts: a genus, which is like your last name, which you share with other relatives, and a species name, which is like your first name.

So if you want to talk about the American Robin, *Turdus migratorius* is the name that scientists would recognize all around the world. By the way, the scientific name for all humans is *Homo sapiens*.

Solstice, summer The longest day of the year when the Northern Hempisphere is pointed most directly at the sun; in the Northern Hemisphere it occurs June 20-22.

Solstice, winter The shortest day of the year when the Northern Hemisphere is pointed furthest away from the sun; in the Northern Hemisphere it occurs December 20-23.

Species name All living thing have a unique scientific name made up of two parts: a genus name, which is like an organism's last name which it shares with other related organisms, and its species name, which is like its first name. See Scientific name.

Toxic Poisonous

Venomous An animal capable of delivering a toxin (venom) through a sting or a bite; rattlesnakes, bumblebees, and jellyfish are all venomous.

Vertebrate animals All animals that have a backbone.

QUICK QUIZ ANSWERS

Page 6, Get to Know California's Biomes

KLAMATH MOUNTAINS

NORTHERN COAST RANGES

SACRAMENTO ●

SIERRA NEVADA

CENTRAL VALLEY

SOUTHERN COAST RANGES

MOJAVE DESERT

TRANSVERSE RANGES

SONORAN DESERT

PENINSULAR RANGES

QUICK QUIZ ANSWERS

Page 9: A. 4; B. 2; C. 5; D. 1; E. 3

Page 11: 1. Spruce; 2. Redwood; 3. Bristlecone;
4. Juniper

Page 13: Answer C, All have been killed or they otherwise
no longer exist

Page 15: A. Pelagic; B. Estuaries; C. Intertidal

Page 17: Answer F, All of them

Page 18: Answer D, All of them

Page 21: Answer D, Cow

Page 45: Answer E, All of the above

Page 50: Answer D, All of the above

Page 76: 1. House Finch, 2. Northern Flicker, 3. Curved-bill
Thrasher, 4. Great Blue Heron, 5. Red-tailed Hawk

Page 82: Answer F, All of them

Page 86: B. Honeybee (A. is a Flower Fly and C. is a Spotted
Tylosis Longhorn Beetle)

CROSSWORD ANSWERS

Page 67, Geology, Gemstones & Fossils Crossword

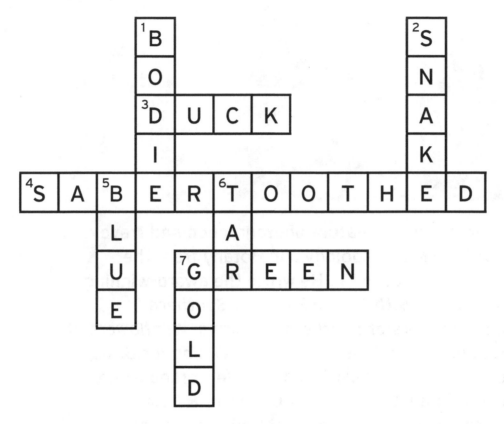

Page 93, Bugs & Insects Crossword

ABOUT THE AUTHOR

George Miller is a writer, nature photographer, and travel journalist with an MS in Zoology and Botany from the University of Texas at Austin. He wrote the award-winning books *Landscaping With Native Plants of Southern California*, *Wildflowers of Southern California*, *Wildflowers of Northern California*, and *Native Plant Gardening for Birds, Bees & Butterflies: Southern California*. He worked as an interpretive naturalist for the Austin Nature & Science Center, where he designed and taught middle school classes on wildlife and day camp programs. He has lived in California, Arizona, New Mexico, and Texas, and is a member of the Native Plant Societies of California and New Mexico. His website WildflowersNM.com covers more than 600 species of Southwest wildflowers, with descriptions, identification tips, and photos.

ACKNOWLEDGMENTS

On our many trips of discovery to the outdoors, my son and daughter, Koda and Heather, helped me see the mysteries and magic or nature with fresh eyes.

DEDICATION

This is dedicated to my grandchildren Colvin, Holden, and Armstrong, that they will learn to love the amazing riches of the natural world.

PHOTO CREDITS

All photos are copyright of their respective photographers.

Front and back cover images used under license from Shutterstock. Front cover: **BenT101**: California Poppies; **next143**: binoculars; **photomaster**: California Quail; **romiri**: scissors; **Sergio Sergo**: ruler; **Vitaly Korovin**: pencil
Back cover: **yhelfman**: California Hairstreak Butterfly

All images copyright by George Miller unless otherwise noted:

Brett Ortler: 70 (top), 71, 80 (leafhopper), 101 (both), 102 (all), 107, 108 **NASA, ESA and AURA/Caltech**: 105; **Fallon Venable**: 99, 114-121 (Background Illustrations).

Images used under license from Shutterstock:
Agnieszka Bacal: 19 (California Quail); **Albert Russ**: 19 (benitoite); **alslutsky**: 19 (California Dogface Butterfly); **Anastasiia Malinich**: 26 (top); **Anatolich**: 81 (cricket); **Andriy Blokhin**: 60 (top); **Andriy Kananovych**: 68 and 69 (all); **Art_girl**: 65 (benitoite); **Asif Islam**: 105 (Milky Way); **barmalini**: 42 (cheese); **Bob Pool**: 82 (pillbug); **bogdan ionescu**: 98 (Chocolate Tube Slime Mold); **Brian A Wolf**: 76 (House Finch); **brizmaker**: 61; **Clark Ukidu**: 70 (bottom); **Contadora 1999**: 42 (flowers); **CORNU Laurent**: 21 (jackrabbit); **dabjola**: 95 (milk mushroom); **Digoarpi**: 96 (Turkey Tail); **dlove**: 18; **Don Mammoser**: 76 (Great Blue Heron); **Ekramar**: 73; **Felix Lipov**: 11 (Bristlecone Pine); **FotoLot**: 97 (False Morel); **Franck Boston**: 38 (almonds); **Garrett Gibson**: 20 (starling); **godi photo**: 96 (puffball releasing spores), 98 (Wolf's Milk Slime Mold);

Henri Koskinen: 95 (russula); **Ilias Strachinis**: 20 (American Bullfrog); **itor**: 42 (pistachios); **Jay Ondreicka**: 81 (Black Widow Spider); **Jennifer Bosvert**: 87 (Mason Bee); **Jillian Cain Photography**: 60 (bottom); **Johnny Adolphson**: 47 (Mount Whitney); **ju_see**: 89 (top); **kakteen**: 96 (puffball); **Ken Griffiths**: 81 (Wolf Spider); **Keneva Photography**: 48; **Lian van den Heever**: 20 (Domestic Honeybee); **luis2499**: 81 (cockroach); **Lusine**: 11 (redwood pine cone); **Maarten Zeehandelaar**: 95 (Green-gilled Parasol); **macrowildlife**: 19 (Native Gold); **Marc Goldman**: 20 (House Sparrow); **MarcelClemens**: 65 (Native Gold); **Matt Jeppson**: 19 (Desert Tortoise); **Michael Rosskothen**: 19 (Augustynolophus morrisi); **Michael Siluk**: 92; **Mike Laptev**: 62; **Nadia Young**: 46; **nechaevkon**: 82 (Dog Tick); **New Africa**: 42 (almonds); **Paul Reeves Photography**: 87 (Mining Bee); **Protasov AN**: 89 (bottom); **Rabbitti**: 76 (Northern Flicker); **ranchorunner**: 76 (Red-tailed Hawk); **robertsre**: 42 (walnuts); **Sarah2**: 79 (House Fly); **Sasha Samardzija**: 19 (Saber-toothed Cat); **Schwabenblitz**: 5 and 127; **Sergey Nivens**: 25; **sezer66**: 85 (top); **Shulevskyy Volodymyr**: 36 (cherries); **Simone Hogan**: 75; **SomprasongWittayanupakorn**: 81 (termite); **SUCHARUT CHOUNYOO**: 82 (centipede); **Sundry Photography**: 110; **Svitlyk**: 97 (Coral Fungi); **Tim UR**: 36 (peaches); **Tomasz Czadowski**: 97 (Morel); **Tomasz Klejdysz**: 80 (treehopper); **VAlekStudio**: 41 (oranges); **Valentyna Chukhlyebova**: 66 (bottom); **Vankich1**: 20 (Yellow Starthistle); **vvoe**: 19 (Serpentine) and 66 (top); **Warpaint**: 65 (*Augustynolophus morrisi*); **Wildnerdpix**: 11 (Coastal Redwood) and 16 (bottom); **Wilfred Marissen**: 76 (Curve-billed Thrasher); **xynabs**: 95 (King Bolete); **yhelfman**: 40 (rattlesnake); **Zikatuha**: 72

NATURE JOURNALS FOR KIDS
from
ADVENTURE PUBLICATIONS

- Guided journaling pages
- Fascinating information
- Fun activities for the family
- Photo and art pages

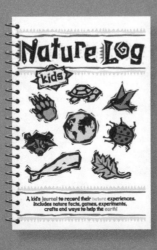

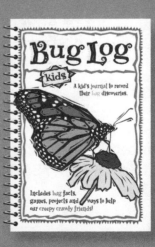

SAFETY NOTE

Nature is wonderful and amazing, and it's certainly nothing to be afraid of, especially if you use common sense and take precautions. This guide is intended for backyards and green spaces in California. These places should be pretty safe by definition, but make sure to have an adult with you when you're outside to supervise the activities in this book. And when you're outside, don't reach where you can't see, and be aware of potentially dangerous animals like bees, wasps, ticks, venomous spiders or snakes, and bothersome plants such as poison ivy.

There really aren't all that many dangerous creatures or plants, but if you know they can be found in your area, or if you have allergies (to bees or poison ivy, for instance), it's important to simply be aware that they may be out there. The best way to stay safe is to keep your distance from wild animals and avoid handling wildlife. Take photos or draw sketches instead. Also, wear gloves, the right clothing for the weather, and sunscreen (as needed), and pay attention to the weather and any potentially unsafe surroundings. **Remember:** You're responsible for your safety.

An especially important note: Don't use this book to help you identify which wild plants, berries, fruits, or mushrooms are safe to eat. Please leave the berries, fruits, and mushrooms you find for the birds, critters, and the bugs. Instead, get your snacks from the fridge!

Edited by Brett Ortler

Cover and book design by Fallon Venable

Backyard Science & Discovery Workbook: California
Fun Activities and Experiments That Get Kids Outdoors
Copyright © 2021 by George Oxford Miller
Published by Adventure Publications
An imprint of AdventureKEEN
310 Garfield Street South
Cambridge, Minnesota 55008
(800) 678-7006
www.adventurepublications.net
All rights reserved
Printed in the United States of America
ISBN 978-1-64755-168-1

CPSIA information can be obtained
at www.ICGtesting.com
Printed in the USA
JSHW050923140521
14644JS00003B/3